739.2 - H38s

Henderson

S

Silver Collecting
for
Amateurs

Silver Collecting

for

Amateurs

JAMES HENDERSON
C.B.E.

Distributed By
SPORTSHELF
P. O. Box 634
New Rochelle, N. Y. 10802

FREDERICK MULLER LIMITED
LONDON

12 8298

First published in Great Britain in 1965 by
Frederick Muller Limited

Printed and bound by C. Tinling & Co. Ltd.,
Liverpool, London and Prescot

Copyright © 1965 James Henderson

4.10-67 *Spottshelf* 4.50

Contents

128200

Illustrations

I

Why Collect Silver?

'*August 7, 1664.* Showed my wife, to her great admiration and joy, Mr. Gauden's present of plate, the two flaggons, which indeed are so noble I can hardly think they are yet mine.

'*November 28, 1666.* Reflections upon the pleasures which I at best can expect, yet none to exceed this; eating in silver plates, and all things mighty rich and handsome about me.

'*April 8, 1667.* but Lord! to see with what way they looked upon all my fine plate was pleasant; for I made the best show I could, to let them understand me and my condition.'

SAMUEL PEPYS, *Diary*.

FEW COLLECTORS are as candid as the Secretary to the Admiralty; but all would admit, if pressed, that they shared his profound personal pleasure and satisfaction in their collections. It is only to be realized by possession; you may view and admire the collections of others, but it is only in your own that real personal felicity is felt. Even the defects of your own collection are of interest. Of course, there are many things you may collect, and feel the same pride and joy, even to dirty little bits of paper that have been through the post; but silver has some attractions.

There is the sheer beauty of the metal itself, and the exquisite shapes into which it may be wrought. Except for gold and precious stones there is nothing in which the mere material can so please the eye. Its lustrous white is wholly delightful and the surface, perfectly smooth yet with a perceptible cling on the finger, is a perpetual pleasure to handle. Apart altogether from value or rarity, silver is a charming substance with which to surround yourself. You have only to compare old silver with stainless steel; the harder metal has every utilitarian advantage, but pleasure, no.

The ductility as well as the beauty of silver has made it a favourite medium of the artist-craftsman throughout history, and long before recorded history began. Before the Pyramids were erected there were many generations of masters of the craft, and today there exist ornaments which were twice as old in Cleopatra's time as Cleopatra's diadem would be for us. There is no known time in this country when there were not silversmiths; and since the commencement of dated hall-marking we can reckon twenty generations of masters, all registering their marks at Goldsmith's Hall. No other collector can cut so wide a swathe in Time, to be reckoned not in decades or in centuries, but in millennia.

The sytem of hall-marking, so jealously guarded and strictly enforced by Governments and Guilds alike, adds a special interest to the collecting of silver. Apart from forgery and some other circumstances (to be explained later) and provided the marks are legible, it is possible to tell with certainty where a piece was made and when since 1478; and since 1697 the name of the maker, too. It is true that there are other objects of collection, such as china and pewter, often bearing marks of interest to the collector of such things; but there is nothing to prevent any potter or pewterer putting what marks he please on his products, so long as he does not contravene the comparatively recent Trades Marks Act; whereas the hall-marking of silver has been most strictly regulated since 1478, ordained by Act of

Parliament and carried out by sworn officers under the super-vision of powerful guilds; and *any* kind of fraud with hall-marks is a felony and at one time punishable by death.

For the English collector there is a further satisfaction: the silver that lies nearest to him is generally acknowledged to have no superior in the world. From the remaining speci-mens it is clear that the Renaissance English silversmiths had nothing to learn from Benvenuto Cellini, and at every subsequent period their works generally surpass those of their continental coevals. In particular, in the great age from 1685 to 1740 all that was best in French was added to the best of the English in producing for a rich and critical aris-tocracy those superb masterpieces which are the final prize of every collector. In no other art does England lead the world. For carpets one turns to Persia, for tapestries to Flanders; Reynolds cannot be ranked with Raphael, nor Etty with Rubens; even our master cabinetmakers fall short of the *ébénistes* of Paris, Chippendale at his best does not equal Cressent, nor Sheraton approach Riesener; but the English silversmiths are universally acknowledged to have no superiors. One is collecting at the fountain-head.

Collecting silver is not a poor man's hobby, although, as will be shown, it is perfectly possible for people of quite modest means to acquire a very satisfactory collection; money is involved, and it must be seriously considered. Is it an irrecoverable expense, like wine, women and song, or a serious investment like land or stocks?

It is fair to say that old silver, purchased with knowledge and prudence, forms one of the very best investments it is possible to make. The purpose of this book is to impart the knowledge and inculcate the prudence.

In the first place, the masters who made silver are dead. The quantities assayed are known. There is not the slightest possibility of some vast unknown hoard coming in to flood the market; quite the opposite. The supply is continually diminishing, by the accidents of fire, theft for melting down, legacies to museums and purchases by them, formation of entailed collections and so on. On the other hand, the demand is continually increasing, here, in Europe and particularly in America, as those who have acquired money acquire taste. One is therefore operating in a market where the increase in value of one's investment is almost automatic.

This has been the case over the centuries. No matter what the state of the money market or the stock market, the value of old silver has gone on steadily increasing, faster during inflation, slower during deflation, but always increasing. An occasional panic, as in 1929 or 1931, may set the market back a little; but that is when the long heads buy.

When Samuel Pepys bought bits of silver—'a fair tankard, which come to £6 10s. at 5s. 7d. per oz.'—'I paid for a dozen of silver salts £6 13s. 6d.'—he was not thinking of a long-term investment; he was buying because he liked to 'have all things mighty rich and handsome about me', and he had great pleasure in them during a long lifetime. Today they would be sold, at the very least, for a hundred times what he paid. Only if he had bought land in the muddy hamlet of Knightsbridge could he have made a better investment.

In 1947 a private collector bought at a public auction in Edinburgh, well attended by dealers, a George I coffee-pot for £92. Fourteen years later he sold it to a well-known firm in London for £280. This was no 'special bargain', no private transaction in which someone might be persuaded to sell too cheaply or to buy too dearly; it was bought in front of the trade and sold to the trade. Had the same sum of money been invested in Government stocks at that date it would, at the time of sale, have been worth about £40. True, the collector did not have the £3 a year or so the stocks would have brought him, but the pleasure he felt every time his coffee was poured was worth much more than tuppence a day. Of course, it is not always that gilt-edged falls so far, nor silver appreciates so quickly; but we live in an inflationary period, and there is the hard fact of actual experience. If this little capital had been put into gilt-edged stock, half of it would have been lost in fourteen years; put into antique silver, it trebled its value in the same time.

This is the happy position of the collector of old silver. He surrounds himself with objects of great beauty, intrinsic worth and practical use, always increasing his domestic pleasures and the respect of his friends. He looks around him with artistic delight and financial complacency, knowing that every year his treasures are increasing in monetary value, while meantime he draws rich dividends of pleasure and satisfaction.

2

The Metal and how it was worked

THE WORD 'metal' is not a scientific term, but everybody knows what they think it means. The ancient world recognized six metals, gold and silver (the 'noble' metals), copper, tin, iron and lead (the 'base' metals). The alchemists of the middle ages recognized mercury as a metal and assigned planets to each, silver being Luna. Much earlier, in Roman times, there appears some mystical relation between the metal and the moon, probably due to the apparent colour of the satellite.

Silver is an element, symbol Ag. It has an atomic weight of 107·9, which may be compared with aluminium 27·0, copper 63·6, gold 197·3, and uranium 239·6. Silver is a better conductor of heat and of electricity than any other metal, it melts at 954°C., which may be compared with 233°C. for tin, 1045°C. for gold, 1054°C. for copper and 1775°C. for platinum. It is the second most ductile of metals, the first being gold, which can be beaten into sheets so thin that there are 250,000 to the inch. Silver is not nearly so ductile, but can be beaten into leaves of 1,000 to the inch, approximately the thickness of electro-plating. It can be drawn into wire 1/1000th of an inch in diameter.

Silver occurs naturally in veins and nuggets, which have been reported weighing several hundredweights and even tons, and no doubt it was thus that it was first discovered and used; but in prehistoric times the art of extracting the metal from ores was discovered, and a process is described by Pliny in which the ore is washed several times in succession and then melted together with lead, much the same process that is now called cupellation. Asia minor appears to have been the principal source of silver in ancient times, in Roman times Spain and Sardinia. Tacitus mentions gold and silver as products of Britain. In the middle ages the principal European sources were the mountains of Germany, and the lead mines widely distributed. After the Conquest of Mexico and Peru vast quantities of silver flowed into Europe through Spain, and over some centuries the interception of a Spanish treasure-ship was a favourite pastime of armed mariners, from plain pirates like Drake and Dampier to the frigate captains of Nelson's time operating under the Articles of War. These prizes made a very considerable addition to the country's supply of silver. As one example, after the capture of two Spanish frigates in 1799, the silver was conveyed from Plymouth to the Bank of England in 63 ammunition waggons.*

Today Mexico, U.S.A. and Canada are much the largest producers of silver. Of a world production running about 276 million ounces a year, North America accounts for 212 million ounces, of which 75 million ounces is from Mexico. Most of this production goes into the treasury of the United States.

While there is a certain amount of ore and lode mining, most of the silver is obtained as a by-product of lead production. The proportion varies, but usually 50 to 80 ounces of silver are produced along with each ton of lead.

The value of silver in terms of gold has changed greatly through the ages. Some archaeologists have said rather vaguely that at one time silver was more valuable than gold, but giving no authority that I am aware of. Baikie has said

* The four frigate captains involved had £40,000 apiece as prize-money. At that time their regular pay was under £200 a year.

categorically of the loot taken by the Egyptians after the battle of Megiddo in 1480 B.C. that the silver was then 'scarcer and more valuable than gold'; but this seems highly improbable for the period, only a few centuries before the time of which the chronicler triumphantly relates that silver was nothing accounted of in the days of Solomon. All evidence points to the probability that gold and copper were the earliest metals used, and that at some prehistoric time when silver was first produced it may well have been the scarcest and most valuable metal. The earliest definite knowledge is a decree by King Mena, of the First Dynasty of Egypt, fixing the ratio at 2½ of silver to 1 of gold, and the relative value of silver seems to have declined steadily ever since that date, about 3400 B.C. In the time of Pliny the younger, about A.D. 100, the ratio was 10 of silver to 1 of gold, and a decree of Constantine of A.D. 334 fixed it at 14¾ to 1. From the Middle Ages to the beginning of this century it was fairly constant around 20 to 1; and at present it is about 27 to 1. This progressive change in relative value is consonant with what is known of production and demand of both metals. At the present time the prices of both are arbitrarily fixed by Governments according to their economic ideas or necessities. The price of silver (about 9s. 3d. per oz. in 1964) is for all practical purposes fixed by the Treasury of the United States, as being enormously the greatest market, so that the price at which they are willing to buy becomes automatically the world price.

Silver is always measured by weight, and many different terms have been used in its long history. A fairly comprehensive set of tables is given as an Appendix. Biblical students will note that a shekel is a little more than half an ounce, and a talent nearly a hundredweight, while the Greek and Roman talent was rather more than half a hundredweight and the mina almost exactly a pound. In this country up to 1526 silver weight was expressed as pounds, shillings and pence, the shilling being one eighth more than half an ounce troy; on the date mentioned Troy weight was established as the only legal measure, and it has remained so ever since. It had already been in use for more than a century in this country, having been introduced from Troyes in France. Troy weight, which is used for gold and silver, must be carefully differentiated from avoirdupois, which is used for everything else. The pound avoirdupois is 7,000 grains, and is divided into 16 ounces of 437½ grains. The pound Troy is 5,760 grains, and is divided into 12 ounces of 480 grains. At the present time the pound is never used, and whatever the quantity silver is always expressed as so many ounces Troy. The collector must be able to weigh in Troy. Sets of weights for balances are available, and are desirable in shops or salerooms, but the spring balance is much handier and (unless mishandled) surprisingly accurate. They are generally available in a range of capacities, from 100 ounces by ½ ounce to 4 ounces by pennyweights.

Pure silver is too soft for practical purposes, and it has always been the custom to alloy it with copper, the amount of alloy being a matter of strict legislation over many centuries. The present standard of 11 oz. 2 dwts. pure silver and 18 dwts. copper was laid down in A.D. 1300 by an Act of Edward I and has remained in force ever since, except for a brief period—1697 to 1719—when a higher standard was enforced. In Scotland the standard was laid down by an Act of 1457 at 11 ounces pure to 1 ounce of alloy, which remained until 1720 when the English standard was adopted. The Act of 1300 was valid in Ireland. Many Acts have been passed since, all with the intention of preventing fraud by the goldsmiths, by insisting on marking and the appointment of responsible persons as assay masters. The penalties were gradually increased, from twice the value of the silver improperly hall-marked, to death under a George II Act of 1757. Any kind of fraud with hall-marked silver is still

highly felonious and visited with similar penalties to counterfeiting coinage.

In assaying, the assayer scrapes a little silver from every
part of the article, taking no more than eight grains from
every twelve ounces, four grains to be put in the diet box
and four allowed for losses in testing. The test piece is
either melted with lead in a 'cupel', a small porous crucible,
until only pure silver is left, which is weighed against the
original weight of the scraping: or more usually nowadays
it is assayed by the 'wet' method, in which the scrapings are
dissolved in nitric acid and the degree of purity ascertained
by the quantity of ammonium sulphocyanide required to
precipitate all the pure silver. When satisfied that the silver
is of the proper purity the assay master will authorize its
hall-marking. The silver put in the 'diet box' is allowed to
accumulate, and at regular intervals is melted down and
the bulk again assayed to prove the average standard of all
the pieces assayed, and this silver becomes the property of
the assay office. It will be understood that in a large assay
office such as Birmingham there is a considerable staff, and
the assay master is a sworn officer of high status.

Silver is no longer used in Britain for currency. About
a third of the silver imported is used for silverware, the
remainder in industry. Photographic materials use a very
large quantity, and there is an increasing use in the electrical
and electronic trades. The printed circuits which have so
simplified the assembly of television and radio sets are
printed in silver ink. When used in bearings for rotating
machinery, silver is three times less liable to seize than
Babbit metal, and it is therefore widely used where long
reliability is a more important consideration than cost,
such as aircraft engines and Diesel locomotives. In 1944
the United States Treasury released a thousand million
ounces of silver for these purposes.

The word 'silver' is very frequently used in combination

Right, bell-shaped, silver gilt salt-cellar and cover, 10 ins. high. James I, London 1613. Maker: I.M. *Below*, silver gilt sugar-basin, made from Charles II porringer. London 1686

Above, Charles II porringer, chased and repoussé, of the pre-Huguenot period. $3\frac{1}{4}$ ins. in diameter. London 1676. Maker: T.L. *Below*, Charles II spice-box, typical of the plate produced between the Restoration and the Huguenot influx. London 1676

with some other word, to denote an ore, a compound, or something which might look like silver but is not. These expressions will be found in the Glossary.

The methods of working silver have varied little during the period in which we are most interested, consisting of a few simple tools and the skill and experience of the craftsman. 'By hammer and hand all arts do stand.' It is not necessary to describe the hammers, chisels, gravers, and so on; the only tool which requires explanation is the 'snarling iron'. This is a long bar of steel, a yard or more, which has one end fixed in a vice or built into a wall, and a hammer-head wrought on the other end. This is used to beat out the inside of a vessel which is otherwise inaccessible to the hammer. The hammer-head is inserted into the vessel and placed carefully on the spot which is to be beaten out; the bar is then struck with the hammer of the worker and on the rebound the hammer of the snarling iron strikes a corresponding blow inside the vessel. The weight of the blow and the point on the bar where it is struck are matters for the skill of the hammer-man. With tools thus simple were fashioned all the masterpieces we treasure.

The first incursion of the Industrial Revolution into silver-working was the invention of the flatting mill, for which John Cook took out a patent in 1727. The mill was little used, however, until developed in Birmingham in the 1740s, after the patent had expired. In this process sheet silver of any desired thickness was produced by passing it between a succession of rollers, annealing frequently by heat. This had many advantages. It could be done by unskilled or semi-skilled labour, without the great labour and skill involved in swaging out a sheet with the hammer. The silver sheet was smooth and flat, without the hammer-marks which required to be rubbed off laboriously. Lastly, the sheet had all the original ductility of the metal, whereas the process of hammering tended to make it rather brittle.

B

The next advance was using these sheets by spinning them to shape on the lathe, on a suitable mandrel, whereby one man could produce quite a large number of bodies in the time a craftsman would take to hammer one into shape.

The power-press enabled the ductility of the metal to be exploited to the full, and in Birmingham every kind of simple shape was pressed which could be received between a male-and-female pair of moulds. Towards the end of the century the invention of really hard steel enabled the manufacturers not only to press the shape but also to emboss or pierce it at the same operation. Buttons in particular were turned out in enormous numbers and soon quite large and elaborate pressings became available.

By the middle of the eighteenth century the process of die-casting was coming into use, in which a set of hard steel moulds could be used over and over again, producing sharp casts every time, very different from the laborious methods of casting with wax and plaster.

When the rolling-mill was invented, little mills were made to roll out ribbons of silver, one edge having any required pattern impressed upon it, gadroon, bead, bar-and-bead; no labouring any more with files and chasers.

By 1770, Matthew Boulton, of Birmingham, had a ware-house in London where London silversmiths could purchase ready-cast legs and handles, needing only a little work to clean out, ready-made bodies for every kind of domestic silver-ware and ready-made edges. A little work with the soldering-iron and you took your work to Goldsmith's Hall to be touched with the London marks and your mark as the maker; the total cost being about one-third of that of producing the job by hand throughout.

It is for this reason that in later chapters I break off at 1760. Before that period, certainly before 1740, practically all silver was worked by hand alone, using the simplest possible tools, and the design was entirely the craftsman's.

That is one of the reasons why early eighteenth-century silver is so highly prized. After this date one may be pretty sure that some part at least of the ordinary articles of domestic use was mass-produced at Birmingham, whatever the town or maker's mark. This did not apply, of course, to the more important pieces, which were not wanted in quantity, and also were much more expensive to tool-up. There were also quite a number of well-known makers who never used the ready-made parts and their works are correspondingly sought after today. It is not difficult to distinguish, once you have seen a sufficiency of examples, but it is extremely difficult to describe in words. What, in words, is the difference between a hand-made button-hole and a machined one? You must begin by comparing any piece made before 1730 with a similar piece made after 1780, preferably a Birmingham piece which is sure to have as many ready-made parts as possible; and as you go on, never missing an opportunity of comparison, you will in time be able to distinguish at a glance. The first ten years is the worst.

Note: Further reference to the rise of machinery is in Chapter 7.

3

Historical

ARCHAEOLOGISTS ARE abandoning the classification of
several Stone Ages, followed by a fairly short Bronze Age
and then an Iron Age, and it becomes increasingly apparent
that between the Neolithic Age and the Bronze Age stretched
a long Chalcolithic Age, during which the three metals
were known and used but when weapons and tools were
fashioned from stone, for the excellent reason that none of
the metals was sufficiently hard. Copper tools and weapons
have been found but rarely. The three metals were found
quite extensively in rivers, in veins and in nuggets throughout the Middle and Near East at that period. Tin, however,
is scarce and hard to extract. It requires a high standard of
science to know that these hard black rocks can yield a
white and fusible metal, and to furnish ships and men to
explore the world. The nearest source of tin was Cornwall
and Herodotus in about 450 B.C. calls Britain the Tin
Islands. It is easy to understand that as soon as tin became
available (about 1600 B.C. perhaps) everybody would bring
in their obsolete copper weapons and tools to be melted
down with the new metal to be re-cast as the highly desirable bronze; hence the scarcity of copper artefacts. It is
quite certain that for thousands of years before the Bronze
Age gold, silver and copper were well known and worked
with superlative skill by craftsmen using stone tools. It is
a pity that 'Stone Age' has become synonymous with

primitive savagery; in fact such stone as flint, obsidian and diorite can be fashioned into tools of the most delicate precision.

With such tools were wrought the gold bracelets of the queen of King Zer, of the first Egyptian Dynasty, perhaps 3400 B.C., perhaps much earlier; and the magnificent silver vase which Entemna, the patesi of Lagash in Sumeria, presented to the local god about 2850 B.C. This has two bands of ornament, one representing cattle, the other the Eagle of Lagash grasping two lions in its claws. Conception and execution show the complete master and it is obvious that such perfection of technique could only be reached after centuries of evolution of the craft.

Silver and gold melted together form electrum, which was much used in ancient Egypt. In the campaign of 1478 B.C., 'His Majesty went forth in a chariot of electrum, arrayed in his weapons of war.' Even in the very beginning of Egyptian history we are told that King Mena made a great oblation of electrum for the fourth time. With its pale green-yellow colour, electrum does not generally commend itself to the modern eye, but there is no doubt that it was a favourite with Egyptian craftsmen.

Discoveries in Mycenae, Crete and Antolia have shown conclusively that over a wide area of Europe and Asia the art of the silversmith was practised by a great number of workers of the highest proficiency before 1400 B.C. In Mycenae alone the contents of only two graves (the first discovered) of gold and silver articles of the finest workmanship is catalogued in 115 pages, one example being a life-size ox-head in silver with gold horns and 56 small replicas in gold.

Many people are inclined to treat the Biblical stories of the gold and silver of Solomon as merely fable, but there is no reason why it should not be accepted as fact. The quantity of treasure which David amassed for the Temple in a prosperous reign of forty years, supplemented by a much larger contribution from the people, amounted to about 10,000,000 ounces of gold and 20,000,000 ounces of silver; a substantial amount, but the silver is only 2 per cent of the quantity issued by the U.S.A. in a single year for aircraft engine bearings. The three hundred shields which Solomon made would have to be fairly thin if they were to be eighteen inches across. Solomon's annual income would amount to rather less than ten million pounds today, about the sum which a city like Birmingham extracts from its ratepayers for local purposes, a revenue which has been exceeded by private citizens both of the Antonine Age and our own, and less than half the annual donation of a slightly later King of Egypt to a single temple. There was plenty of gold and silver about in 1000 B.C., and plenty of smiths to fashion it magnificently.

When the fair-haired heroes of Homer descended upon Mycenaen Greece, they destroyed all trace of that civilization so thoroughly that everybody believed her legends to be myths, until the God-inspired grocer Schliemann began his excavations in 1870. Yet in a few centuries this barbaric race became the most civilized people the world has ever known, and the next two thousand years were spent in trying to recapture the artistic, philosophic and scientific impetus of the fifth century B.C. Under the patronage of Pericles and the direction of Pheidias, the Parthenon was built to house the colossal statue of Athena, forty-five feet high and covered with gold weighing more than 30,000 ounces. Later, the same artist made the colossal golden statue of Zeus at Olympia, which must have exceeded his Athena in size for it was reckoned one of the Seven Wonders of the World. When such things were done in gold, what must have been the production of the thousands of silver-smiths, in an age when an Athenian could scarcely put pen to paper or chisel to stone without producing a masterpiece?

At the same period, in the earliest days of Republican Rome, silver and gold were so scarce that they were almost unknown and currency was reckoned by the *as* of copper (about a pound Troy). A citizen had to be worth more than 100,000 *asses* to qualify for service at his own expense in the heavy-armed infantry of the legions. At a later date one ounce of silver was the equivalent of seventy pounds of copper or brass. The Pyrrhic wars and the loot of the Greek cities of Southern Italy first brought the Romans in contact with the art of Hellas, and the Punic Wars brought a great influx of silver as war reparations. After the first war, and the Sardinian affair, the total exacted was 4,400 talents, which (if Greek talents, a smaller weight) would exceed three million ounces. After the second war Carthage was to pay two hundred talents for fifty years, a total of over seven million ounces.

After the wars in Greece, Asia and Egypt the treasures of art of all the known world flowed into Rome, nor was there any need to melt them down for currency; the mines of Spain provided an ample supply of fresh metal. The bronzes of Corinth were almost equally valued as the silver-ware of Antioch and Alexandria. The Saepta Julia was the Bond Street of Imperial Rome, where imported treasures were purchased by bargain or by auction; but hundreds of silver-smiths plied their craft in the City itself. The roof of the Capitol was plated with over ten million ounces of gold and the quantity of silver used for domestic purposes was al-most incredible. Every respectable citizen had all the equip-age of table and toilet of silver, and we read of great bed-steads of massive silver, finely wrought. Martial pours scorn on niggardly patrons who did not give more than sixty ounces of silver-ware apiece to each of their clients at Saturnalia. Pliny complains of the drain to India of perhaps three million ounces a year of silver, the principal means of paying for the silks and perfumes for Roman ladies; but nevertheless the available silver continued to increase in quantity and decrease in price.

The Empire fell apart and was thoroughly looted by Goths, Huns, Vandals, Arabs, Moors, Mongols and Turks. The extent of the treasure is perhaps best guessed at by the booty taken, not from the City itself, but from provincial towns of small account; the Toledo gold dish of five hundred pounds weight; the hundreds of large gold vessels of the church of Narbonne; five hundred thousand pounds weight of silver vessels from the Cathedral of Syracuse; the life-size statue of Hercules, in solid gold, from Heracleia. All the treasures of the Empire vanished from Europe. Where it all went to, who took it, where it might be now, 'though puzzling Questions, are not beyond all Conjecture' which might be pursued elsewhere. Probably it is in the treasuries of India. The certainty is that throughout Latin Christendom silver was very scarce, gold seldom seen and the art of the silversmith almost forgotten. In France the silver mines continued to be worked after the Frankish irruption, but even so the Merovingian kings appear to have struck coins as coronation medals rather than as an ordinary medium of exchange. The scarcity appears to have been worse after the age of Charlemagne, when the heathen Hungarians and Normans ravaged inland and littoral Europe respectively; they respected not the altar, and it is notable that the Abbey of St. Denis could provide 685 pounds of gold for the ransome of its Abbot, at a time (A.D. 860) when King Charles the Bald had the greatest difficulty in raising three thousand pounds of silver for the defence of the realm. It is interesting that withing a hundred years the Kingdom of Hungary and Norman Kingdom of Naples and Sicily should have become the bulwarks of Christian civilization against Turk and Saracen. Which comes first, silver or civilization?

So scarce were the precious metals, and coinage so frequently debased by needy monarchs, that the Byzantine byzant, or besant, about half a sovereign, became the principal circulating gold coin of Europe, and the Persian Dinar, Moorish Markish (thus the mark) became the usual coin of account. It is during this period that the Jews came into prominence as financiers. Their contact with Arabs, Moors and Byzantines; their reliance on what was virtually a paper currency and their complete confidence in each other, all were completely foreign to the Northerners and enabled them to transmit large sums of money in security without transporting bullion.

Constantinople, the bulwark of Christendom, was sacked by the Crusaders in 1204 and the loot made an appreciable increase to the precious metals of Western Europe; but the scarcity still continued and a little later the whole revenue of the Kingdom of France amounted to 72,000 pounds of silver. The crowns of even the most potent monarchs were merely slight circlets of gold. The craft of the silversmith revived in spite of, or perhaps because of the scarcity of the metal; the more precious it was, the more labour one might bestow in working it. When the final overthrow of Constantinople was clearly only a matter of time, the Byzantine craftsmen as well as scholars began to make their way to Italy, where they were welcomed by Popes and princes to found the Renaissance school of goldsmiths. They were still handicapped by the scarcity of their metals. Gold and silver began to flow into Spain early in the sixteenth century from the Indies,* but only slowly permeated the rest of Europe. Benvenuto Cellini, the greatest known goldsmith, was always projecting works and making models which his patrons received with great applause, but unfortunately they had not the necessary silver. True, he did make for Francis I of France the great gold salt-cellar which is still extant, but

---

* It has been estimated that between 1500 and 1820 Spanish ships carrying treasure made 17,000 voyages from America to Spain, with a total value of £4,000,000,000 sterling.

he made only one of a set of twelve life-size silver statues which he projected, although Francis almost ruined his subjects by his extortions to further his splendid ideas. As supplies of the precious metals increased, so did the craft of the goldsmith, which like all other arts reached one of its highest peaks during the great outburst of humanity we call the Renaissance.

4

English Silver before 1660

THERE IS no doubt that gold and silver were mined in England before the Roman occupation. Tacitus mentions gold, silver and other metals among the products of the Island, 'to make it worth conquering'. Silver was probably obtained by the Romano-British in connection with the extensive production of lead, but where gold was found is a mystery. After the withdrawal of the Legions there is a period of centuries which is almost a complete blank. We know much more about Egypt in the fifteenth century B.C. than about England in the sixth century A.D. It is certain, however, that the warlike Saxons would preserve the craft of the armourer, and the hammer-man can also fashion silver. It is related that in A.D. 793 the bones of St. Alban were discovered and Offa King of Mercia had the skull encircled with a band of gold and the bones deposited in a box inlaid with gold and turquoises. It is said that the wealth of England was an inducement to the mercenaries who flocked to the banner of William the Conqueror, and the Bayeux Tapestry depicts Harold wearing a handsome regalia. It may be accepted, however, that the possession of articles of gold and silver was restricted to the Crown, principal ecclesiastical bodies and the great Earls.

I am not aware of the name of any Saxon goldsmith before the Conquest. The earliest name is that of Otto the Elder, graver to the Mint in 1090, who was followed by Otto the

Younger and then by William FitzOtto. These are obviously
Normans. Contemporary with them appears the Saxon name
of Leofstane, but all other goldsmiths mentioned in the
next two centuries appear to be Norman. Henry FitzAylwyn,
goldsmith, was the first Lord Mayor of London, in 1189,
and held that office for more than twenty years. In 1181 a
number of goldsmiths in London were fined for having
established themselves into a guild without Royal authority.
But the growing craft required regulation to protect the
public against the use of excessive alloy and in 1238 the
goldsmiths of London were required to appoint six of
their number to superintend the craft, and in particular to
see to the standard of silver used. In 1300 their authority was
confirmed and they were ordered to assay every piece of
plate and, if worthy, to stamp it with the leopard's head.
The London goldsmiths were regularly incorporated in
1327 and their status was enhanced and defined by an Act of
1462. The following year another goldsmith, Sir Philip
Matthew, became Lord Mayor.

The provincial smiths were also active. In 1423 an Act
provided for a system of hall-marking in York, Newcastle
on Tyne, Lincoln, Norwich, Bristol, Salisbury and Coventry.
The omission of Chester is curious, for the craft had been
established in that town two centuries before and was then
active. From 1314 to 1414, eighty goldsmiths became free-
men of the city of York. Of the towns named in the Act the
first four had flourishing guilds at the time, but in the case
of the last three there is no evidence worth noticing that
they ever operated as guilds at all. In Tudor times the most
productive provincial towns were York, Norwich, Exeter
and Chester, Norwich being noted for the excellence of its
workmanship, 'equal to that of London'.

Probably the most important Act of Parliament relating
to goldsmiths was that of Edward IV in 1477, which established the present system of hall-marking and re-enacted

the standard of silver already laid down. Successive Acts have reaffirmed or modified this Act, but the general principle has been strictly observed from that day to this. In a part of the Tudor period the silver coinage was grossly debased, so much that in 1551 the coinage was only one-quarter silver and three-quarters alloy; yet the standard for plate never varied. One of the earliest Acts of Queen Elizabeth I was to restore the currency of the Sterling standard, which remained until 1921.

The period of the Tudors and the early Stuarts was a prosperous time for the silversmiths, as may be judged by their numbers. In the 150 years before 1484 the names of less than 150 London silversmiths are known; in the 150 years following, more than a thousand, including four Lord Mayors. The dissolution of the monasteries and the breaking-up of the lands of most of the great old families put wealth into the hands of considerable numbers of 'new men'. The Tudors liked display, and they liked their favoured subjects to 'make the best show they could'. Earthenware was crude and fragile, glassware an expensive import, pewter despised; it was silver that furnished every table, from the modest citizen to the Royal household. According to Sir Philip Warwick, every cobbler in London drank out of his silver beaker, 'so rife were silver vessels among all conditions'. The extravagant courtiers of James I were liberal patrons of the silversmith, and Charles I was the only English monarch who was a true connoisseur. The quality of the work has never been excelled in any period or any place; most surviving examples are quite equal to the known work of Benvenuto Cellini. The standing salt, a foot high, of the Vintner's Company, London 1569, shows the complete mastery of craft and design. The Goldsmith's Company, among much other treasure, has the Bowes Cup, 19 inches high, from which Queen Elizabeth I drank after her coronation. Hall-marked London 1544, it was presented by Sir

Martin Bowes, goldsmith, possibly to mark the first of the six times he was Lord Mayor. Earlier are the Leigh Cup of the Mercer's Company, height 16 inches, hall-marked London 1499; the standing salt of All Souls College, Oxford, 17 inches high, probably 1460, and the Foundress's Cup of Christ's College, Cambridge, 13 inches high, about 1440. These last two examples were before the Act of 1477 established the system of the date letter.

These are only examples; it is certain that the landed gentry and nobility, many of whom were very rich men, would not be outdone by associations of tradesmen or teachers, and contemporary references to the splendours of plate displayed by various notables leaves no doubt that by 1640 England was a treasury of Renaissance silver. Ten years later it had gone. The whole plate of England was melted down and made into coin, to arm and pay troops, and later to pay ruinous fines. As early as 1635 Cromwell asked a friend 'Who goeth to warfare at his own cost?' When the King removed to York in March 1642, the royalists came in with their plate, while at the same time the citizens of London contributed their plate to the Parliament 'even to women's thimbles'. On 15th August, 1642 the House of Commons noted that 'Mr. Cromwell . . . hath hindered the carrying of the plate from that University: which, as some report, was to the value of 20,000 *l* or thereabouts'.

> *Did Saints for this bring in their plate?*
>
> .   .   .   .   .   .
>
> *And into pikes and musqueteers*
> *Stampt beakers, cups and porringers?*

There were 140,000 recruits to pay, arm and equip, plus a Scottish army whose *arrears* of pay by the end of 1646 was £200,000. The nation had only one reserve to meet this emergency—its plate. The pressure for silver money was unceasing. The only relief was when Blake captured a Spanish plate-fleet and sent 38 waggon-loads of silver from Portsmouth to the Tower, where it was immediately coined. This relief was such that Cromwell decreed a day of National Thanksgiving.

What was saved from the holocaust? A few pieces in the hands of the City Livery Companies or Colleges, some coco-nut cups and ostrich egg cups, in which the mounts had little intrinsic value, a few apostle and other christening spoons, a number of trivial cups and vessels too light to be of much melting-down significance and a very limited amount of Church plate. Nor was there any production during the period of the wars and commonwealth to replace what was lost. The very few silversmiths who remained in business were turning out communion plate of the plainest description, small cups and tankards and plain spoons. So small was the production that Sir Charles Jackson spent years seeking examples to complete the tables of London hall-marks for his great work 'English Goldsmiths and their Marks'; and in the case of the provincial guilds there are many years for which no single example could be found.

The cataclysmic destruction of plate; the tiny production between 1640 and 1660, and the remainder being in hands which are most unlikely to let go, are the three facts that rule the market in silver of early date. This is the reason for the stir in the saleroom when there is put up some trifling little wine-taster, marked 1654 perhaps, which would attract no attention had it been made a hundred years later. It is not merely a matter of being a little older; it belongs to a different epoch.

5

London Silver from 1660 to 1760

WE NOW enter the modern age of silver, and from 1660 onwards there is a substantial and increasing production of all kinds of silverware. It has had its vicissitudes, but there has been no wholesale melting-down of plate in Britain. Changes of fashion, and contempt for the styles of previous generations, have been the main reasons for melting down old-fashioned silver which would have become treasured antique three generations later. There has also been a steady drain by sale abroad, especially to America, for it is generally recognized that the work of the London silversmiths of this period had no superior anywhere in the world.

Much of the silver of this period was gilt, not only to give it a handsome appearance but to protect it from the tarnishing caused by the increasing use of sea-coal, both domestically and industrially. The chimneys built to burn wood did not suit coal, and great quantities of sulphur-laden smoke belched not only from the chimneys into the outer air but also from the fireplaces into the rooms. The prevailing winds being south-west, residential building extended ever westward. Greenwich Palace, the favourite residence of Elizabeth and James was turned into a sailor's hospital and Windsor became the Royal palace most in use outside of London. In 1663 Sir Edward Ford, an eminent projector of the period, took out a patent for curing smoking chimneys, the first of many during the next three centuries.

Right, a fine pair of Queen Anne candlesticks, $7\frac{1}{4}$ ins. high, with cast bases. London 1713. Maker: William Twell. *Below*, William and Mary bleeding-bowl, one of a pair, $5\frac{1}{4}$ ins. in diameter. London 1691

Left, an exquisite George I coffee-pot, in great demand during the early eighteenth century. *Below*, hexafoil waiter, 10 ins. in diameter, on three feet. Salvers of this age and condition are rare. London 1721. Maker: Samuel Wastell

The process of gilding silver is very different from the ordinary gilding, in which the surface is covered with gold leaf, applied with an adhesive. To gild silver, gold is dissolved in aqua regia, a mixture of nitric and sulphuric acids, and an amalgam is made with mercury. This is painted on to the silver, which has been heated to a dull red heat. The amalgam eats into the silver, the mercury, under the heat, unites with the acids and goes off as vapour, leaving the pure gold bitten into the silver, in fact an integral part of it. The mercury fumes are extremely deleterious, causing serious diseases of the jaw and eventually death. In the middle of the eighteenth century the practice was gradually discontinued until it was superseded in 1840 by the electro-gilding process. Fire-gilding, as it was called, was nevertheless a very much better process, except for the unfortunate operator. It was so usual that it was taken for granted, and articles which had *not* been gilded were referred to in inventories as 'white plate'. There are many cases known where the gilding has been removed, to please the current taste and perhaps for the value of the gold, and sometimes the gilding has been worn off in the course of use.

From 1660 to about 1730 silver gilt has a very beautiful and distinctive colour, but after that period it became common to apply a thicker coating so as to resemble gold; it was doubtless a distaste for imitation that led to its fall from fashion. Pieces are also found 'parcel-gilt', that is partially gilt, usually having the decoration gilt and flat surfaces left plain; such pieces are highly prized. A more utilitarian form of parcel-gilding is the inside of cups and bowls; these are usually referred to as being 'gilt inside', the term 'parcel-gilt' being reserved for pieces in which it is part of the decoration. All silver-gilt of this period is keenly sought and highly priced.

The demand for silverware began immediately after the Restoration and was not easily satisfied by the existing

C

smiths. It is easier to make revolutions than to make silversmiths. The first demand was for articles of everyday use,
and these the existing smiths could very well supply. In the
course of use these would become damaged sooner or later,
and being of no special interest would be sent back to be
re-fashioned. The most usual piece of this period is probably
the tankard, and William Gamble appears to be the most
prolific maker. The maker's marks of this period are well
known, and so are their names, but it is by no means easy to
identify a mark with a maker. Candlesticks and wall-
sconces, not so vulnerable to the domestic rough-and-
tumble, are to be found, but it is highly probable that the
more elaborate pieces were imported from Holland or from
France. It is difficult to be positive, as silver made to Royal
order was not required to be hall-marked; sometimes it has
only a maker's mark and sometimes nothing at all. It is
certain that the 23-piece toilet service made for the wedding
of Princess Mary to the Prince of Orange in 1677 was produced in France. It was probably from that country came the
silver furnishings which John Evelyn saw in the dressing-
room of the Duchess of Portsmouth, the King's French
mistress, in 1683—'great vases of wrought plate, tables,
stands, chimney furniture, sconces, branches, brasseras, etc.,
all of massive silver.' The massiveness is attested by a
surviving specimen, a pair of wall-sconces 17 inches high
by 13 inches wide weighing nearly 300 ounces. It is
unlikely that the London silversmiths could have produced works of such importance at that date. The splendid
silver table presented a few years later by the Corporation
of the City of London to William III, weighing more than
7,000 ounces and now in Windsor Castle, bears the mark of
Andrew Moore, of Bridewell; but it has very much the
appearance of a composite work. The exquisitely modelled
grotesque caryatid legs suggest French design and workmanship; the over-elaborate stretchers and bun-feet are distinctly

Dutch, while the superb engraving of the top is charac-
teristically English. It seems probable that the worthy Moore,
having been entrusted with the order, obtained the various
pieces from the sources best able to supply, assembled them
and applied his mark as the silversmith responsible for the
whole. This is very common practice at all periods and in
many trades, and there is nothing remotely fraudulent about
it; but the lack of artistic unity would seem to disqualify this
table from being 'amongst the finest silver furniture existing
in any country', as a most respected authority has named it.

The year 1685 marks the beginning of the greatest epoch
of English silver. Louis XIV repealed the Edict of Nantes,
by which Henri IV had established religious toleration.
400,000 citizens left France, mostly to Holland or England.
Most were skilled craftsmen, not tied down like the land-
owners to their possessions and able to earn their bread
anywhere. Many were silversmiths and for the next thirty
years most of the greatest names in the London craft are
French. The emigration went on for many years. In 1689,
to finance his wars of expansion, Louis XIV and his court
melted down all their plate, so that the goldsmiths of France
found themselves in the same position as their English
fellows in 1642—their occupation gone.

Long after the first emigration there was a steady stream
of workers in England seeking the encouragement they
could not find in France. The first comers were welcomed as
religious martyrs, but later a certain resistance built up.
Some difficulties arose about admitting them into the
Company and having their marks registered, and in 1713
a complaint was made that London makers bought the work
of the refugees—'necessitous strangers whose desperate
fortunes obliged them to work at miserable rates'—took
the work to Goldsmith's Hall and had it assayed under their
own marks.

The first wave included Pierre Harache, Daniel Garnier,

Pierre Platel, Mark Paillet, Louis Mettayer and David Willaume. Later came Augustine Courtauld, Abraham Buteaux, Simon Jouet, Louis Laroche, Simon Pantin, Phillip Rainaud, Aymé Videau and Paul Lamerie. Their example and competition stimulated the native masters, such as Anthony Nelme, William Gamble, Ralphe Leake, Jonathon and George Lambe, George Garthorn and John Bodington. Together they founded such a school of master craftsmen as has never been surpassed in any place or at any time in the world's history.

The shortage of coin was a chronic problem in Britain. Under William and Mary various Acts were passed to restrict the export of silver and its too wide use; one Act prohibited inn-keepers and taverners from having any plate in their house except spoons. At length an Act was passed, effective from 25th March, 1697 (25th March was New Year's Day at that time) which had an important effect. It provided that any hall-marked silver should be purchased by the Mint at 5s. 4d. per ounce. It raised the standard of purity of plate from the ancient standard, 11 oz. 2 dwt. pure to 18 dwt. alloy, to a new standard of 11 oz. 10 dwt. pure to 10 dwt. alloy. It instituted an entirely new hall-mark, a figure of Britannia and a lion's head erased, to mark the new standard and it introduced a new system of maker's marks. Hitherto, makers had made what mark they pleased, so long as they acknowledged it. From now the mark was to be the first two letters of the surname, with or without any other symbol at the maker's pleasure; and these marks were to be recorded at Goldsmiths Hall, with the maker's name and address opposite his mark.

This Act was not intended for the benefit of collectors yet unborn, nor to improve the standard of wrought silver. It was simply a device to make it more difficult to convert the coinage into plate, to encourage plate to be brought into the mint, and to make it easier to identify makers in case of

breach of regulations. It was also intended to help the
infant Bank of England, whose notes were regarded as
much less acceptable than the note of a substantial merchant,
and stood at 20 per cent discount. The ultimate effect,
however, was to establish the system of marking which still
prevails, by which any maker can be positively identified if
his mark is legible; the form of mark has varied, but the
record remains. At the period under discussion, however,
there is a wide possibility of error. In 1719 another Act was
passed, preambling that the higher standard of silver was too
soft for ordinary use and therefore legalising the old sterling
standard. Workers in this standard were to use a new mark,
consisting of the initial letters of the Christian name and
surname, or alternatively the mark used before 1697; but
those who preferred could go on using the Britannia standard with their mark as registered in 1697. Confusion grew,
and at last in 1739 an Act was passed ordaining that all
makers should destroy their existing stamps and henceforth
use only one mark consisting of the initials of Christian and
surnames, whatever standards of silver was worked. Since
that date there has very rarely been any difficulty in ascertain-
ing the maker of any London plate.

The background reason for the legislation restoring the
sterling standard was that the Bank of England had got
over its teething troubles and its notes were now readily
acceptable everywhere in the country, so that there was no
need to use law to conserve the silver at the disposal of
Government. Confidence in Bank paper became synonymous
with confidence in Britain, so that in 1760 Lady Harrington
tipped off Casanova that he was committing a social solecism
by paying his gambling losses in gold; paper was the done
thing. This confidence in paper currency had, of course,
very wide economic results when the rest of the world was
still in the bullion age, not the least being the full availability
of silver to the English silversmiths without restriction.

The Britannia period brought many changes in the style of plate. The softer quality was too weak to use in the same way as the sterling; to add strength, fluting was introduced; coffee-pots became octagonal instead of conical; all vessels were more elaborately worked and shaped, not so much for the ornamental effect as for strength. In the hands of consummate artists, however, this elaboration was used with the utmost taste and restraint, and this period is generally regarded as the summit of the craft.

All this changing of marks, with alternatives, raises difficulties for the collector, which are increased by the date letter for the cycle 1697 to 1715 being in 'court hand', very difficult to decipher after it has endured the wear of two and a half centuries. Then it was found that far more people have the same first two letters of their surnames than have the same initials; hence the return to initials, largely stultified by permissive exceptions. More errors are liable to be made in this period than any other, and every circumstance has to be carefully considered before decision. Thus in the marks registered in 1697, of surnames beginning Ga, we have William Gamble, Daniel Garnier, George Garthorne, and a GA surmounted by a mitre to which nobody has been able to attach a name. To make it more difficult, both Garnier and Garthorne used two forms of mark.

Even more difficulties arise in the case of Paul Lamerie, who many consider the greatest of them all and who in recent years has been called de Lamerie. It is not known why, for none of these Huguenot tradesmen claimed to be anything else than honest bourgeoisie. Lamerie would appear to have been a son of an early immigrant and apprenticed to Paul Platel, an eminent Huguenot silversmith. Quickly showing himself a master of the craft, he married the boss's daughter and entered his own mark in 1712, LA with a crown above and a fleur-de-lis below. He did not re-

register in 1720 but kept on working Britannia standard
until 1732, when he registered PL, also with crown and
fleur-de-lis. In 1739 he registered pl in italics, with a crown
above and a dot below. Now during the beginning of his
LA period there was a small tradesman called John Ladyman,
whose mark was LA with a crown above; there was also
George Lambe, who registered LA with a lamb above and
a dot below, Thomas Langford, who registered LA with a
dog above, and the widow Lambe, with a mark similar to
that of her late husband. It might seem difficult to confuse
a crown with a lamb, but when one considers how small
these marks were and that they were struck in very soft silver
and almost obliterated by the wear of centuries, an error is
easy; add a little wishful thinking and one can very easily
believe that one's piece by George Lambe is actually by
Paul Lamerie and worth three times as much, although not
necessarily of better quality.

In his PL period there is sometimes confusion with his
father-in-law, Pierre Platel, whose mark at one time was PL
also with a crown above and fleur-de-lis below; also the PL
with a fleur-de-lis below of Gabriel Player and the PL ringed
with dots of Francis Plumley. All these PLs, however, are
of a date when Paul Lamerie was using LA. There was also
in Exeter Richard Plint, whose mark was PL with a crown
above and a dot below; but he also used this mark earlier,
and in all human probability had discontinued it before
Lamerie registered PL. Thus if the date letters and the maker's marks are quite legible it is easy enough to identify
Lamerie's work from that of his contemporaries; but often
enough the marks are so worn that they can only be seen at
all by breathing on them and, before the mist departs,
looking at them sideways in a strong light. One might be
guided by the craftsmanship and importance of the piece
but in fact very many contemporaries worked to equal standards, and in his younger days Lamerie made sauce-boats

and salt-cellars like anybody else. Identification is important, for in the eyes of almost all collectors a piece by Paul Lamerie is indeed a prize.

It is impossible to understand the passion for silver plate among all classes at this period, unless one compares it with the passion for motor cars which intoxicates the present generation. There were many reasons. In the infancy of banking, silver afforded the safest means of storing capital—under one's own eye and immediately convertible if required. It was also a status symbol. The great cistern on the sideboard was the Bentley, the massive wine-cooler the sable. In an age when bribery was universal but manners more refined, the present of plate replaced the pair of gloves lined with ducats. Pepys occasionally bought some small pieces, but most of his splendid sideboard came from presents from Admiralty contractors. Every important officer of the Crown, on taking office, received a vast allowance of plate as a permanent perquisite. An Ambassador, a Speaker of the House of Commons, a First Lord of the Treasury, would all receive at least 6,000 ounces of plate. The first Earl of Bristol was by no means really wealthy for his time, but his account books reveal that he bought more than 20,000 ounces, plus more than 2,000 ounces of his father's plate which he had melted down and re-fashioned.

Apart from their superior taste and skill, the Huguenot masters introduced the new art of casting details of ornament, which were finished with the chisel and graver, giving a sharpness and delicacy that could never be approached by beaten silver. Larger and larger pieces become fashionable, till many a nobleman would have 'ten thousand acres standing on his sideboard'. The Earl of Devonshire had a cistern weighing 3,496 ounces; the Earl of Meath one 3 feet 6 inches high. These are commonly referred to as 'wine cisterns', but many contemporary references show that they simply held water for rinsing plates and glasses.

Wine coolers of this period were also gigantic, consisting of vast oval dishes in which bottles of wine were packed in ice. There are several existing weighing over 3,500 ounces. Pilgrim bottles, the successors of Pepys' 'noble flaggons', were smaller, but seldom less than 300 ounces each, and one among the Royal plate is nearly 500 ounces. Great hanging candelabra, toilet sets, and table services of massive plate bore permanent testimony to the wealth and taste of their owners.

These enormous pieces are very unlikely to come the way of the ordinary collector, and if they were to appear in the salerooms the prices might be a disappointment. Almost all the remaining specimens are in museums, a very few still owned by great old families. The largest pieces which have survived are mentieths, punch-bowls, ewers and basins, but the ones most often found are smaller domestic pieces, tea- coffee- and chocolate-pots, hot water and milk jugs, 'porringers', cruets, candlesticks and salvers.

In the case of salvers it became fashionable to decorate the large plain surface with an engraving of the owner's coat of arms, suitably embellished, and this work was executed with a grace and certainty never achieved before or since.

Artists of repute did not regard silver-engraving as un- worthy of their genius. William Hogarth (born 1697) began in this employment, being apprenticed to Ellis Gamble and afterwards working for Paul Lamerie and others; he was thirty before he painted his first picture, and there is evidence that he was still engraving silver at least occasion- ally after 1730. On a very few pieces his initials may be dis- cerned among the ornament. It might be possible to identify some of his early work by his admiration and professed imitation of the French engraver Callot.

Another engraver who signed his work was the Huguenot Simon Gribelin, who also published books of designs, as did also Joseph Simpson, whose silver-engravings are usually signed. A prolific engraver who did not sign his work was Benjamin Rhodes, whose name is known chiefly because one of his account books has been preserved, from which it appears that he seldom received as much as a pound for the most elaborate heraldic engraving. Fully to appreciate the energy, spirit and variety of the engraving of this period it is necessary to compare it with the dull, lifeless repetitions of the Victorian period.

As the rococo period advanced, ornamentation became more profuse; all was well as long as the style remained in the hands of the masters, but they were dying out, and their places taken by lesser men. Paul Lamerie, the last of the giants, died in 1751, and even in *his* later work there appears a slight confusion of naturalistic ornament, a falling away from the superb simplicity of his prime. The simpler domestic pieces retained a grace, but in the larger works one finds over-embellishment, decoration applied rather than arising naturally out of the main design, weaker drawing throughout. It became quite common for the owners of the old plain plate to have it brought up to date by new elaborate handles, extra embossing, chasing and applied ornaments. Machine-rolled sheet completely replaced hand-beaten. Already some of the smaller London silversmiths were buying ready-made parts from Birmingham, mass-produced at low prices. It was the end of the epoch. The great tide or the Restoration and the Huguenot inflow had spread wide and dispersed itself. It was time for something new. But it had been an illustrious period, the Augustan Age of English silver.

6

London Silver from 1760 to 1914

1760 IS A convenient date for the beginning of the classical revival. George III succeeded to the throne, not that the worthy young man had any influence whatever on taste. Robert Adam came back from Italy, with his drawings of Diocletian's palace at Spoleto, to be appointed Architect to the Board of Works in 1762. An ever greater influence was the fashion for young men of position to make the Grand Tour, accompanied by some learned tutor, for about three years, much of which would be spent in Italy amidst the remains of Rome. Some acquired a taste for gambling and worse, but far more acquired a taste for Roman antiquities.

This was strictly a Roman revival. Almost all the remains of Greek culture at that time were within the Turkish Empire, and few cared to venture into the power of the Pashas. This period must therefore be distinguished from the classical revival of the beginning of the nineteenth century, which was under Egyptian and Greek influences and which, fostered by the prevailing philosophy, had a much more profound effect. So far as silver was concerned, this was an addition of Romano-classical ornamentation to existing styles, rather than a fundamental revolution of ideas.

A second feature of this period is the division between the designer and the craftsmen. Hitherto the artist-craftsman designed his work and carried it out. No doubt the larger

silversmiths employed numerous journeymen and appren-
tices to assist them with the rougher parts of the work.
As early as 1540 Cellini employed up to twenty assistants
in Paris and the prolific workshops of London would use
many more; but every piece was designed by the master and
came under his eye and hand before he put his mark on it.
From now onwards it is much more usual to have the design
drawn by an artist who did not necessarily fully understand
the material in which it was to be carried out. Robert Adam
insisted on designing everything about a house down to its
least furnishing, and his example was naturally followed by
his disciples. The artist-craftsmen of the great days died out
and their successors were merely skilled artisans, carrying
out not only the wishes of their patrons but copying closely
the design supplied to them. No doubt the designs were
excellent and the artisans skilled; but something was lost
for ever.

A third factor was the rise of the English potters. Hitherto
pottery and porcelain was imported from France, Italy and
China. It was not uncommon for an English gentleman to
have a drawing of his coat of arms sent to China, to be copied
for the sole decoration of a large set of dinner-ware. Western
designs on Chinese porcelian are well known to every collector. Large pieces of Majolica ware, and smaller pieces
from Sèvres and Meissen, were usual household decorations.

In this country, Josiah Wedgewood was producing the
most handsome vases imaginable, decorated by excellent
artists in the classical style newly in vogue, while at Derby
domestic ware was being produced in fine porcelain. Dr.
Johnson might well give faint praise and point out that he
could have silver plates at the same price, and much less
fragile.

A fourth factor was the much larger houses which the
Adam school was building for all the squires, classical

structures with many niches to receive the statuary which the heir had brought back from the Grand Tour. Hitherto the main decoration, apart from pictures and furniture, had been the magnificent sideboard of plate, gilt splendour against oak background. Amid the cool, pale-blue elegance of those vast Adam apartments, silver-gilt was a little out of place; demodé; perhaps even a trifle vulgar? It was banished from the salons to the pantry, to be produced when required for service.

Fifthly, there was the great expansion of the manufacture and use of glass. Hitherto largely an import, glassware became an ordinary domestic manufacture, cheap and plentiful. Henceforth it was only on special occasions that sentiment would call for the 'pint of wine' to be filled 'in a silver tassie'; the 'brimming glass' was the toper's expectation. This was stimulated by the increasing consumption of port wine, ever since the Methuen treaty of 1703 and the frequent French wars. One could drink claret, champagne or Rhenish from silver, but port wine, with its tendency to sediment or 'beeswing', was best drunk in a transparent vessel.

Thus it came about that many a gentleman whose grandfather had dwelt in a modest oak-panelled manor, surrounded by magnificent vessels of silver-gilt and being served only on silver, now lived in a vast Adam mansion filled with statuary and majolica, eating from porcelain and drinking out of glass. It was not poverty, quite the contrary; it was that tastes had changed.

The change of taste would not be a matter of regret in the least had it been confined to new silver; but many heirs of the massive silver of the time of William III or Anne sent all this old-fashioned useless stuff to the silversmith, to be melted down and re-fashioned into a large number of useful vessels in the modern-classical style. This we now deplore, but must not blame the owners; it was their own, and they thought no more about it than we now think of the melting-

down of some vast Victorian table centrepiece, which might
—who knows?—otherwise become a treasured museum
piece in A.D. 2170. But it is of interest to note that this period,
say 1760 to 1800, was the last in which there was any large-
scale melting of silver by heirs. Silver became increasingly
available and cheaper, while the cost of working it increased;
the economy was stabilized on a bank credit basis; there was
a demand for old silver; and it was only in the case of hope-
lessly damaged or worn-out pieces that no more could be
had, in financial emergency, than 'melting-down value'.

There is no doubt that the massive pieces of earlier periods
were regarded very much as storage of capital, readily turned
into money. Now there were many and profitable uses for
money. Silver was now used in smaller and lighter pieces,
for the service of the table rather than as status symbols.
There is during this period a very large production of
domestic plate for every possible purpose, comparatively
little of large and massive pieces. Gilding is very seldom
used; 'white plate' was much more in harmony with an
Adam interior.

No master gives his name to the period. There were many
excellent workers but none towering above his fellows.
The names of sons and grandsons of the masters of the
Augustan Age are still found, Nelme, Le Sage, Courtauld,
Calamy, along with the founders of new dynasties, Chawner,
Bateman, Storr, Garrard.

Just as the Adam influence began to fade, a new classical
impetus made itself felt. The French Revolution encouraged
itself with much verbiage about the republicanism of ancient
Greece. The influence spread. There was an almost immediate
and drastic change in dress and furniture. Women who five
years earlier would have felt uneasy without five petticoats
under a heavily-embroidered dress, stepped boldly out in
1795 wearing only two layers of muslin. This was further
stimulated by Napoleon's expedition to Egypt and British

actions in Egypt, the Levant and Sicily, still rich in Greek remains. The classic style spread to everything; to be fashionable was to be *à la Greque*.

In silver, this Grecianism is found mostly between 1800 and 1820, although examples are found both earlier and later. Instead of the applied ornament of the earlier period, the swags and wheatears, the aim of the best smiths was now to produce effect by the pure elegance of line of the article itself, decoration being either entirely absent or restrained to a narrow band of fine engraving, a reeded handle, a double-line edge. There is very little beaten work. Where more decoration was required, the piece or part was cast and then chased, the figures being sharply cut out of the solid and left in relief against a tooled background.

This period, which we call Regency for convenience, was productive of the most beautiful silver now within the reach of the ordinary collector. It was a great age. The wars which desolated Europe did not touch the guarded island, whose inhabitants regarded naval victories and the conquest of empires with the same enthusiasm now accorded cup-tie winners. The Prince Regent, whatever his failings, was the First Gentleman of Europe, unequalled in taste, manners and magnificence, the last true aristocrat to fill the British throne. With exquisite taste flowing down from the throne, resounding victories abroad and the wealth of the world flooding through the ports, it is not surprising that the Regency is one of the great periods in London silver.

There are many well-known makers, and families of makers, in this period. Hester Bateman registered her mark in 1774, Peter and Jonathon Bateman in 1790, Peter and Anne Bateman in 1791, Peter, Anne and William Bateman in 1800, Peter and William Bateman in 1805, William Bateman in 1815, William Bateman and Daniel Ball in 1839. None of this family engaged in very important works, but they had a large production of domestic plate in the best taste of the period. It is not certain when T. & W. Chawner registered their mark, certainly before 1765. Thomas Chawner registered before 1773. William Chawner registered in partnership with George Heming in 1774. The great Henry Chawner entered in 1786. William Chawner entered as junior partner in Eley, Fearn & Chawner in 1808, and on his own in 1815. Mary Chawner and George Adams entered their mark in 1840. Of this dynasty the most renowned was Henry Chawner, who made the Westminster Abbey plate for the coronation of George IV. He had also a large production of fine domestic pieces, and a cake-basket bearing his mark is the most beautiful piece I have ever possessed. The most famous name of this period is undoubtedly Paul Storr, who entered in 1792 as junior partner with William Frisby, and on his own account in 1793. Like Paul Lamerie, it is difficult to account for his pre-eminence over his fellow-craftsmen, but there is no doubt that he was considered outstanding both in his own time and now. He was liberally patronized by the Prince Regent, made many important pieces for him and even got paid eventually. He had a large workshop which turned out a great number of quite ordinary domestic utensils; certainly a pair of his large toast-racks in my collection have nothing about them of a master-hand.

Throughout the whole of the classical period 'pierced work' retained its popularity; and in this style even the most chauvinistic of Continental smiths allows that the London makers excelled. No doubt beginning as fancy designs for the tops of sugar-casters, pierced work in the 1760s was used on cruet-stands, mustard-pots, cake-baskets and all sorts of domestic wares. It blended well with the swags and other classical details of the earlier period and was never completely abandoned throughout the Regency, although it was very little used by the London silversmiths of the Grecian fashion; they left it to Birmingham. Never-

Right, George II coffee-pot, bearing the arms of Caldwell. Renowned artists, such as Hogarth, earned their living by engraving silver. London 1735. Maker: William Kidney. *Below*, George I tea-pot with engraved border on shoulder. London 1726. Maker: George Wickes

George II: *left*, spirit kettle on stand. An excellent example of restrained use of rococo details. London 1746. Maker: J. King. *Below*, cream-boat, typical of the rococo of Paul Lamerie's late period. London 1742

theless, pierced work, a typically English style in which the English excelled, has a very understandable attraction for many collectors, and fortunately the very large production during this period has left a supply commensurate with its popularity.

Comparisons are generally to be avoided, but it is instructive to look at the gilt breakfast set made for Napoleon I on the occasion of his marriage to Marie Louise. This was made by Biennais of Paris in 1809, passed through various hands (including a Duke of Hamilton) and is now in the Louvre, not quite complete. It is impossible to say whether it reflects the taste of the Corsican or the Austrian, but it is a hotch-potch of ill-considered and inconsequent ornamentation. At that same period there were in London a good score of silversmiths who had completely mastered the most complicated of arts—to satisfy the eye completely by form alone.

What is really astounding is that the French style ultimately prevailed, and the successors of the Regency masters competed to pile ornament on decoration, abhorring a plain surface as nature does a vacuum. The fashion for ornamentation increased from about 1825, to reach a shrieking crescendo in the silver shown at the Great Exhibition of 1851. It is dangerous to criticize adversely the art of a preceding century; the century succeeding might take a very different view. Dickens ridiculed the Sheraton style of furniture, Thackeray admitted that painting in England was in a woefully low state at the end of the eighteenth century (Reynolds! Lawrence! Gainsborough!) and preferred Mulready; an eminent architect wrote in 1850 of 'Robert Adams, whose corrupt taste had invented a style which contained all the worst peculiarities of the worst class of ornamentation and composition.' It is, however, safe to say that these elaborated mid-Victorian pieces are totally rejected by twentieth-century collectors. The lowest price I have ever seen paid in an auction-room was for a table centre-piece of this period which might well have merited a mention in the *Art Journals*'s catalogue of the Great Exhibition—a thing a yard high, wrought with figures and foliage, not a plain square inch anywhere and weighing more than 300 ounces. It was bought by an eminent dealer at 1*s*. 9*d*. an ounce, less than half the current melting-down price.

Everybody can recognize on sight a piece of this period; yet there was no period style. Everything was reminiscent, even nostalgic. As the greatest Empire ever known nonchalantly extended itself over the world, its enriched citizens yearned towards a dimly-seen past. The aristocrats were content with Paul Lamerie or Henry Chawner; the rising merchants, emotional, sentimental, demanded that every picture should tell a story; and they could pay. A glance at the catalogue of the Great Exhibition silverware tells all:

'A very magnificent Fontain à Thé, exhibited by M. Durand, of Paris; it is entirely of silver, but by recourse to gilding, burnishing, oxidizing and niellos, a most beautiful variety of effects is produced . . . The various elements of the style are very well expressed—the cinquecento grotesque scroll-work, the scrolled and pierced shields, and the conventional Saracenic foliage in relief, illustrating the origin of Elizabethan strap-work, and . . . the value of the Saracenic element.'

'A gilt vase, with a frieze in relief in oxidized silver, representing a boar-hunt in German Cinquecento.'

'Chiefly in the style of the Renaissance, but with a sufficient mixture of Rococo'.

'Mr. George Angell exhibits . . . a very superior candelabrum, with a lioness defending her cubs against a boaconstrictor.'

At the same time, however, the perpetrators of these

works of art were turning out a great deal of comparatively plain domestic silver which is perfectly acceptable to any formed taste. My own table is set daily with Queen's pattern cutlery made in 1848 by the George Angell aforesaid. I like it; solid and handsome, enough decoration but not too much; no boa-constrictors. There were also tea-pots in a sort of Queen Anne style, fat-bellied, usually engraved but sometimes plain, the latter being very acceptable indeed. As there was no contemporary style every period was imitated, and quite often the imitation is highly if heavily successful.

The inevitable classical revival set in about 1870, and cabine makers toiled to produce vast quantities of Hepplewhite and Sheraton, while the silversmiths contributed their version of Adam. All the way to 1914 there are these imitative designs, of which I rather like the Queen Anne styles and definitely dislike the Adam imitations. Generally the followers of the earlier school are content to make close replicas, while the Adam imitators have some ideas of their own to work in, mostly with disastrous results.

There was one definite period style which evolved at this time. William Morris and his disciples had been labouring away for twenty years in comparative obscurity and suddenly at the end of the century there sprung forth *L'Art Noveau*. It was too shortlived to have any real effect on architecture, but between the deaths of Queen Victoria and the Archduke Ferdinand every European of any pretensions had at least one room completely re-furnished in the New Style. Those who were born in that period are much too near to it to pronounce a confident judgement. Osbert Lancaster, whose opinion must always be respected, considered that 'no style seems at first glance to provide a richer field for the investigations of Herr Freud.' Undoubtedly the style is redolent of the lilies and langours of the *fin du siècle*, but a 1904 rosebowl of mine appears to show a free and confident application of new ideas to mass and shape. If I were advising a collector who wished to lay up treasures on earth for his grandson, I should suggest a lot of *Art Noveau* silver. It is usually plain; at present it can be bought very cheaply; it is a definite style, not imitative of anything preceding, having recognizable origins in Morris and Beardsley; and it has its definite limits in time, ending with a bang—several bangs—in 1914.

Here I cease the record of London silver. I might have said something about modern silver, but 'there is no subject of which I understand so little' as Wellington said about Army uniforms. Kind friends have offered to brief me, and I have the greatest admiration for such firms as Heal's who strive for patronage for the modern artist-craftsman; but I suffer from a total inability to distinguish modern silver from stainless steel, and one must admit one's limitations. Old silver I understand, old silver I love; I restrict myself to old silver.

7

English Provincial Silver from 1660

THE PROVINCIAL guilds never recovered after the Civil Wars. Not only was there a virtual suspension of business for nearly twenty years but political events brought about a concentration of the wealth and influence of the country in London. The cultures which had existed in ancient Roman centres like York or Chester died out. Norwich and Exeter became agricultural market towns, no longer the assembly places of the aristocracy. Everybody who was anybody spent a large part of each year in London, and no provincial city could hope to emulate the guild that was building up there.

So much did the London smiths dominate the English scene that the Act of 1697, introducing the Britannia standard and altering the hall-marks, referred to London only, and the unfortunate provincials were left without any legal status at all; so that three years later a special Act had to be passed extending the Act of 1697 to the provinces, the guilds named being York, Exeter, Chester, Norwich and Bristol; Newcastle on Tyne being added later. Of these, there is no conclusive evidence that any silver ever was assayed in Bristol. The Exeter guild died out in 1697 and was never resuscitated. York had to give up its ancient and most interesting mark, a half fleur-de-lis and a half-leopard's head conjoined, and did not take kindly to the new mark. The guild ceased to operate at the end of Queen Anne's reign, but was more or less revived in 1787. There were very few workers and marking ceased about 1850. Norwich also died in 1697 and its fine marks, a crowned rose and a lion bearing a castle, are seen no more. Newcastle on Tyne took quite well to the new conditions and the craft was actively pursued by a sufficiency of workers for more than a century. It began to fade after 1820, when there were only two families working, and there is little if any to be found after 1840, although the assay office did not close officially till 1884. In its heyday there was a considerable production of silver with the Newcastle mark, although it appears that some was made in other towns, such as Sunderland, and York during the suspension of the office there.

None of these provincial guilds produced a silversmith of note or any works of importance during this period of decay and eclipse. Still, collectively they produced a fair quantity of good ordinary silver, which turns up from time to time, and it behoves the collector to know something about them.

Chester is the only one of the guilds named which has survived to the present day, and this is not so much on account of the activities of the town guild itself as because it stamped gold and silver made in the rising Midland and Lancashire cities—Liverpool, Manchester, Birmingham and others. The craft was a very ancient one in Chester and long before the Norman Conquest coins were being minted there. Names are known of Chester goldsmiths early in the thirteenth century, but there is no identifying town mark until the Charter of 1685, after when a part of the town arms was used—three wheat-sheafs with a sword—and this has been used ever since except for the period 1701 to 1778, when one wheatsheaf was used along with three leopards passant guardant in the same shield. It would appear that prior to 1685 only a maker's mark was used, and it is highly improbable that anyone will ever be able to identify or date early Chester work.

During the eighteenth century the production was small. The family of Richardson was prominent, at least three generations, for they are first heard of in 1701 and last mentioned in 1787; one Richardson was Sheriff in 1714, another Mayor in 1751. It is clear that very few others were actually making plate in the city at that time, and in the century 1780 to 1880 there were more smiths in Liverpool alone, having their wares marked at Chester, than there were in Chester itself. It is probable that the large amount of silver which appears so frequently with the Chester mark, dated between 1890 and 1914, was actually made in Birmingham, but marked in Chester to avoid the faint stigma which some people still attached to the machine-produced 'Brummagem'.

While the guilds were dying out in the ancient cities, there were arising in Sheffield and in Birmingham large numbers of skilled metal workers who were turning their attention to silver. This was viewed with keen jealousy by the London Company, who had been happy to see the extinction of their ancient competitors and who feared the new. The invention of Sheffield Plate stung them to fury, and in 1757 they secured an Act introducing the death penalty for applying marks resembling hall-marks to any other metal than solid and sterling silver. But the new men were not without resources. They were numerous. They were rich, enterprising, energetic. They were already applying in practice the new principle which Adam Smith had not yet formulated as an economic philosophy—the division of labour. No longer was the craftsman to perform the whole work, from the first rough sketch to the finished product. Henceforth the designer, shaper, raiser, chaser and burnisher were to be different men, working for wages under the direction of the enterprising capitalist.

Above all, they were led by that remarkable entrepeneur, Matthew Boulton (1728–1809). Inheriting his father's toy* manufactory, he soon became the leading metal manufacturer in the world. In one factory he made everything from buttons to ormulu mounts, which were praised by Catherine of Russia and widely used by French furniture manufacturers. In partnership with James Watt he made steam engines; when Boswell visited his Soho factory (employing 700 men) he was told 'I sell here what all the world desires —POWER.' In partnership with John Fothergill he made silver-ware, and it was as a silversmith that he organized the Parliamentary campaign to have assay offices established in Birmingham and in Sheffield. In 1773 petitions, supported by a great number of influential persons, were presented to Parliament, on 1st February by Sheffield and on the 2nd by Birmingham. It was represented that owing to the large amount of plate being produced, it was an intolerable burden for the Sheffield smiths to send their work to London and the Birmingham workers to Chester. The Inquiry by Parliamentary Committee was lively. The London Company extolled the extent and perfection of their assay office, to which the petitioners replied that when they had difficulty in getting their plate marked in London all they had to do was to make acquaintance with the junior officers and give them 'drink' (at this time a euphuism for petty bribery), after which they had no difficulty at all. London referred to the scandals of the Sheffield-plate makers applying marks which might resemble hall-marks, to which the reply was that this could best be prevented by having an assay on the spot. The report of the Committee was entirely favourable and an Act was passed expeditiously granting all that was asked for.

Birmingham was given exclusive rights over all silver production within thirty miles radius. A Company was formed, headed by the Earl of Dartmouth and including

* At this period 'toy' meant any small article of personal or domestic use, not a child's plaything. Fans, snuff-boxes, buttons, shoe-buckles, tea-caddies, combs and brushes were sold in 'toy-shops'.

several noblemen, gentlemen and leading citizens as well as silversmiths. Sheffield was given a radius of twenty miles, its Company being similarly constituted, with the Earl of Effingham as Chairman. Its first Assay Master was Daniel Bradbury, the first of a name highly honoured throughout all subsequent Sheffield history. In the next twenty-five years more than 150 makers registered their marks in Birmingham and over 200 in Sheffield, compared with rather more than 200 in London. The Birmingham list was headed by Matthew Boulton and John Fothergill, and there appear such names as James Elkington in 1807, Matthew Dixon in 1815, Freeth & Jones in 1818 and Deakin & Deakin in 1845. In Sheffield there appear Jonathon Mappin in 1775, Charles Roebuck in 1786, William Fox in 1775, Watson, Bradbury & Co., in 1795, Matthew Fenton in 1773, Thomas Bradbury & Sons in 1832 and Mappin & Webb in 1860.

Thus by the beginning of the nineteenth century the silversmiths of Birmingham and Sheffield together outnumbered the silversmiths of London and far surpassed them in productive capacity. This tendency increased. In 1854 an Act was passed which, among other provisions, abolished the former territorial limits and allowed any maker or owner of silver to have it hall-marked at an assay office of his choice. It now became more profitable for London makers to cease actual production in their own workshops, or at least drastically reduce it, obtain their wares from Birmingham and have them assayed in London under their own maker's mark and the London hall-marks. The same slight snobbery kept alive the assay office at Chester, the only other one in England, where most of the silver marked was made in Birmingham or Sheffield. This feeling for having silver made in Birmingham or Sheffield and marked in Chester or London was perhaps due to the fact that the two older guilds were renowned from ancient times for silver, whereas the new cities were open for anything. Matthew Boulton set the course when he wrote in 1767 to his foreign agent that he would 'work for all Europe in all things that they have occasion for—gold, silver, copper, plated, gilt, pinch-beck, steel, platins, tortoise-shell, or anything else that may become an article of popular demand.' This is the authentic voice of the modern enterprising capitalist, far removed from the artist-craftsman.

The same factors operated during the whole of the nine-teenth century, until nowadays Birmingham has almost a monopoly of silver-ware production, Sheffield making more of plated goods and, of course, cutlery. It was all an in-evitable part of the progress of the factory system. The organized team of specialists was bound to turn out a cheaper and often a better article than the craftsman who had to do every part of the work himself as best he could. Thus we find that by the first decade of the twentieth century where we stop, Birmingham is turning out every kind of silver which was 'an article of popular demand', all well designed in whatever style was wanted, well constructed and well finished, not a fault to be found anywhere.

8

Scottish Silver

THE STORY of Scottish silver is very different from that of English. Until 1707, although sharing a king since 1603, Scotland fiercely maintained its independence from England and its connections were much closer with France, the Netherlands and Poland. The many harbours of the Firth of Forth admitted easy sea passage. For generations Scottish gentlemen provided the personal bodyguard of the King of France; later, the Scots Brigade in Holland played no small part in military history. In 1625 a census showed 30,000 Scots resident in Dantzig alone, and at that time Scottish students did their post-graduate work in Paris or Leiden.

Scotland also had a substantial native production of gold and silver, now largely exhausted. In 1153 David I granted to the Abbey of Dunfermline one tenth of all the gold that should come out of Fife and Fothrif. To this day the patient tourist may amuse himself by panning a few grains of gold from certain streams in Sutherlandshire. The chief source of silver was, and still is, the great deposits of lead under the desolate moors of Dumfriesshire. On 23rd January, 1562, John Acheson and John Aslowan had a license from Mary Queen of Scots to work the lead mines there, on condition that they brought into the mint forty-five ounces of refined silver for every thousand stone weight of ore. This is very much less than the modern rate of extraction and it may be supposed that the prudent burgesses had some silver for themselves as well as the lead.

The artistic inspiration was also entirely Continental. In 1536 the Newcastle goldsmiths strictly forbade under penalties any brother from employing either as journeyman or apprentice any 'Scots man born in Scotland', and heavily penalized any such slander as calling another brother a Scot, a murderer or a thief.

Saint Margaret, although a Saxon, was entirely educated at the court of the King of Hungary. When she married Malcolm III in 1068, she caused his table to be served with vessels of gold and silver—'or at least', says the candid Turgot, 'the dishes were gilded or silvered over'. During the Hundred Years Peace the country prospered and even after the long and devastating Wars of Independence the last will of Sir James Douglas of Dalkeith, 1392, included such items as these: 'One broad covered ewer weighing fifteen pounds three shillings and eightpence; my best gilt drinking cup, weighing eighteen pounds two shillings; my best twelve silver dishes, weighing twenty-one pounds eighteen shillings, and one silver charger weighing four pounds two shillings and twelve silver spoons weighing forty-eight shillings; my best drinking cup after the first, with the cover, weighing eight pounds four shillings and fourpence, and they are gilt.'

These are indeed massive pieces and if we may be guided by the remaining pieces of that period the workmanship would be superb. Those who only know Scottish silver by the post-Reformation work can have no idea of its prime in the fifteenth century, illustrated by the three maces of the University of St. Andrews (one made in Paris) and the steeple cup of St. John's Church in Perth. When in 1436 the King's daughter went to France to marry the Dauphin, one of her escorts, William St. Clair Earl of Caithness, was attended by a hundred gentlemen all with chains of gold, and his wife by seventy-five gentlewomen so decorated.

Almost all this magnificence was melted down in 1640

to pay and equip soldiers for the civil wars. In the feudal period every fencible man had to serve forty days at his own expense and with his own weapons, but now the armies had to keep the field for years, and must be paid. Even earlier than in England the plate went. In June 1639 most of the towns ordered 'the haill plait' of the citizens to be brought in and appointed proper officers to see to it. Thus we find in the household accounts of the Countess of Mar this item, without comment: 'Paid for carrying down the silver wark to the Council House, to be weighed and delivered to the town treasurer of Edinburgh, 10s. The disaster was even greater than in England, where new schools arose; the later silversmiths of Scotland, although competent tradesmen, were quite incapable of emulating the works of their fifteenth-century predecessors.

As in England, the capital city was of the first importance, although in the earlier times of difficult communications the provincial towns had greater place than they had later. The first Scottish statute about goldsmiths is that of 1457, which ordains that silver is not to be of worse standard than eleven pure to one of alloy; and that in every town where goldsmiths worked there should be ordained 'an understanding and cunning man of a good conscience' who should be deacon of the craft. Every worker was to put his own mark on his work, and after due probation the deacon was also to put his. In 1485 the town mark was added. Where there was only one goldsmith or none the Town Council was to appoint an officer to mark if required. No date letter was enacted.

The standard of old Scottish silver is thus slightly lower than in England. The establishment of the Britannia standard in England in 1697 did not affect Scotland, which was then a separate kingdom, although under the same crown. The Act of 1720, however, re-establishing the sterling standard, was an Act of the United Kingdom and thenceforth all Scottish silver was of the same fineness as English.

Up to 1730 the Edinburgh marks were as laid down in 1485 and the order of marking never varied; first the maker's mark, then the town mark (the castle) and then the deacon's mark. In the absence of a date letter, it is necessary to ascertain first the period in which the maker was active, and then the period during which the deacon held sway. As some held office for several years, and others were re-elected after a period, it is not always easy to establish a date within a year or two. I was once permitted to examine the Communion cups of Kinghorn Parish, which are ascribed by Bell, in the monumental work 'Scottish Communion Plate', to the year 1651, the deacon for that year being James Fairbairn. I formed the opinion that the mark was more probably that of John Fraser, which would put the year at 1642. Fortunately the Kirk Session minutes were still extant, and a search put the matter beyond doubt. In 1642 the Session borrowed two hundred pounds (Scots) from the Poor's Fund to pay for the new Communion cups. This sort of supporting evidence is very desirable if one is to be positive about the exact date of early Scottish silver.

In 1681 an assay master was appointed to mark instead of the deacon, John Borthwick being the first Master, with only four successors in the next eighty years. At the same time a date letter was adopted. In Edinburgh the sequences went right through the alphabet, making a cycle of 25 years, i and j being the same except in 1814 which is i and 1815 which is j. In 1759 the assay master's mark was discontinued and a thistle struck instead; since then the mark has been Maker, Castle, Thistle and Date, with the addition of the Duty Mark (the Sovereign's Head) from 1784 to 1890.

In the Scottish provinces the craft was scantily manned. In 1688 there were 25 goldsmiths in Edinburgh, 5 in Glasgow 3 in Aberdeen, and 1 each in Perth, Inverness, Ayr, Banff and Montrose. In addition, there are undoubted marks of Tain, Wick, Elgin, Greenock and Dundee, and others which are

ascribed by excellent authority to St. Andrews and Stirling.
Only in Glasgow was there a significant production continu-
ing to the present day. All the other marks have long since
ceased and it is very unlikely that the collector will find
anything other than spoons with these marks. In the case of
the small northern towns such as Tain and Wick it is probable
that the work was not that of resident goldsmiths but
itinerant tinkers, hammer-men of skill, who made coinage
into spoons and brought them into the burgh to be stamped.
There is an extraordinary variety of marks even in the same
town and the earnest student must seek fuller information
in the copious pages of Sir Charles Jackson. It is perhaps
scarcely worth the trouble for the Southern collector for it
is rarely that anything except Edinburgh plate will come his
way; but in Scotland I have several times picked up 'lots' of
spoons or toddy ladles at tiny prices, because the 'trade'
thought that the unfamiliar marks denoted plated stuff.

Early eighteenth-century Edinburgh silver has a great
deal of charm, but the best period is the end of the century
and the beginning of the eighteenth, when a great deal
of excellent silver was produced; domestic pieces, for
generally when an important piece was required it was
ordered from London. There is no outstanding master, although some families are very well represented, such as Ker.
Thomas Ker was admitted in 1694, Robert in 1705, James
in 1723, another James in 1737, William in 1760 and Daniel
in 1764. I have seen a bullet-shaped tea-pot by Robert Ker,
1724, offered in a shop at £24: happy yesterday!

As the nineteenth century progressed and Glasgow became the second city of the Empire, more silver is to be found
with the Glasgow marks. In 1819 a lion rampant was ordained, no doubt in place of the lion passant of the English
marks; and in all periods the town's emblem has been struck
—a somewhat complicated mark consisting of a tree with a
bird sitting on top, a bell hung from a branch and a salmon

suspended across the trunk; I believe the salmon should have a ring in its mouth. When all this is reduced to three-sixteenths of an inch in height, not all the detail is readily perceived. Before the establishment of the assay office in 1819 comparatively little plate was made in Glasgow and the marking was very irregular. After this date there is a regular sequence of date letters, the whole alphabet being used in a cycle of 26 years. All the ordinary plate of the nineteenth century was produced in great profusion, but there is nothing that calls for special remark.

The Scottish Renaissance silver is out of the reach of the ordinary collector. The silver of the end of the seventeenth and beginning of the eighteenth centuries is quaint and interesting rather than splendid, contrasting unfavourably with the London work of the same period. The best Edinburgh silver to look for is between 1760 and 1830, when the Athens of the North had a cultured population of demanding taste.

Top, sauce-boats, London 1762. *Centre*, sauce-tureen, typical of the later rococo style. London 1764. *Bottom*, tray-shaped ink-stand with pierced galleries. London 1773

George III: *left*, candel
abrum, one of a pair. The
classical style, under Adam
influence. London 1789
Maker: John Schofield
Below, tray, 21 ins. long
A fine example of en
graving used throughou
the eighteenth century
London 1791. Maker
Joseph Heriot

9

Irish Silver

IRELAND HAD probably in early times large native supplies of gold and silver. Where the gold mines were is not known, but practically every early example of decorative skill is in gold. The silver mines not far from Cork were worked in comparatively recent times, and it would appear that anciently the craft centred round Cork and Youghal rather than in Dublin. In history, however, Dublin is far more important than all other Irish towns together; goldsmiths are named there as early as A.D. 1200 and there is mention of a guild in the fifteenth century. In 1557 the City Council granted a renewal to the goldsmiths of their charter, which they said had been accidentally burnt. To what extent Dublin 'within the pale' was a beleaguered city is shown by the clause that nobody was to be admitted to the Guild 'without he be of English name and blood'. In 1605 the City Council established a mark and in 1637 Charles I granted a charter to the goldsmiths of Dublin, giving them much the same powers and duties as their fellow-craftsmen of London.

There are few guilds better documented than that of Dublin, but none with so few remaining examples of their skill in earlier days. Most of the existing plate was melted down by Order of Council in 1642. Cromwell brought the Civil Wars in Ireland to a pitch of exterminative ferocity unknown in England and while the Revolution of 1688 was bloodless in England, in Ireland it was fiercely contended

E

during three years of war and seven more of armed resistance. The records show that the craft was practically extinguished; between the charter of the guild in 1637 and the 'pacification' of 1693, scarcely forty pieces of plate remain. What is surprising is the rapid recovery and the high quality of silverware produced. Ireland, like London, had its proportion of foreign immigrants, and no doubt these had the same beneficial influence, as little appreciated at the time; one brother was called before the court of the guild for the crime of having employed a Frenchman. By 1700 26,000 ounces a year was being assayed and the figure rose to 60,000 by 1725; this average was maintained and often increased until 1820, when there was a sharp fall. In 1835 only 6,000 ounces were assayed and production has remained almost negligible. In 1903, 30,000 ounces were assayed, which may be compared with the 3,790,000 ounces assayed in Birmingham that year, more than a hundred times as much.

There is thus a reasonably substantial if limited production during the best period, 1720 to 1820, and Dublin silver is highly prized, not only for its relative scarcity but for its uniformly high standard of execution. No maker has achieved individual fame above his contemporaries; Charles Leslie, a Scotsman admitted in 1723, is said by excellent authority to be 'not inferior to Paul Lamerie', but I have not come across his work. The most typically Irish production of the period is the dish ring, very often called a 'potato ring', of pierced work very well designed and wrought. These dish rings are much sought after and the collector must be prepared to pay a good price for any that appear on the market. The pierced work of the latter half of the eighteenth century is also prized, but all the production of the period 1720–1820 is excellent, equal to the average London work of the same period.

The Dublin hall-mark has in all periods been the crowned

harp, along with the maker's mark. After 1730 the figure of Hibernia was added, probably to denote that the duty of sixpence an ounce imposed in 1729 had been paid. In 1807, immediately after the Union of the Parliaments of Ireland and Great Britain, an Act of the United Kingdom was passed imposing the same duties in Ireland as elsewhere, and ordaining the Sovereign's head to be stamped as a duty mark. This did not, however, supersede Hibernia, which has been stamped on all Dublin silver from 1730 to the present day, along with the crowned harp, while the Sovereign's head was dropped when duties were repealed in 1890.

The Dublin Guild is perhaps the best documented of all whose records remain, but it does not appear certain that the officers pursued their duties with the same enthusiasm as they kept their records. There is no lack of ordinances, which may be taken as indicating that they were not being observed; for in the 'most distressful country' passing an enactment and getting it carried out were two different things. There are a number of prosecutions, which might show zeal on the Warden's part or simply the frequency of the offences. Fines and forfeitures were entirely for the benefit of informers. The sixpence duty seems to have been strongly resented and it is not at all uncommon to find plate which has apparently been made between 1730 and 1780 which has no date stamp; without this it would be difficult to *prove* that it had been subject to duty and this omission could only have been with the connivance of somebody in the Assay Office, unless all the marks were counterfeited by the silversmith. It certainly appears that the use of counterfeit marks and the transplanting of marks from old pieces was by no means uncommon. Where this can be discovered it does not mean at all that the silver is below standard; it only means that both the silversmith and his customer were anxious to avoid paying the obnoxious tax.

The Dublin Guild was the only regularly chartered guild

in Ireland, with the full powers to assay, mark or reject silver and to discipline the craft. These powers extended over all Ireland and much silver bearing the Dublin mark was, in fact, made in the provincial towns. It would appear, however, that this was done principally when the owner wished to use the silver in Dublin or take it into Britain, when he would risk confiscation if it had not an official set of hallmarks. By accepting some unofficial mark he would save the costly and hazardous journey to Dublin and back, and also avoid the hated sixpenny duty. In Cork and Limerick were excellent silversmiths who could do anything with silver except strike the official marks; they were by no means inferior to the workers of the capital. Both cities had their quota of skilled immigrants, such as Charles Bekeagle, and also natives like the three generations of the name of Goble: silver bearing their marks is usually prior to 1720 and is highly valued.

In both Cork and Limerick, from about 1720, it was the regular practice to mark silver only with the maker's mark and the word 'Sterling', the spelling being varied occasionally. There is also to be found sometimes the word 'Dollar', indicating no doubt that Spanish coin had been melted to produce the plate. Before 1720 there exists plate of Cork, Limerick, Youghal and Galway, and probably other towns bearing town marks which can sometimes be identified, but this early plate is so scarce and the marks so various that it is not worth space to dwell on it; it is very unlikely to come the way of the ordinary collector and if a piece were to turn up in the saleroom it would be fully discussed in the catalogue. There is, however, a fair supply of the 'Sterling' mark and it is always of interest, although naturally difficult to date precisely. Limerick silver will usually be found as tableware, but a number of quite important pieces were made in Cork in the eighteenth century, although later the production tails away into the usual spoons. There is very little of the 'Sterling' mark after 1815, though silversmiths are known in both towns up to about 1850; but if they were actually operative they would no doubt have their work marked in Dublin, the more settled state of the country making it both safer to send it and more dangerous to evade duty.

There are a number of pieces of plate, apparently of Irish origin, bearing marks which it is difficult to ascribe to any town or maker with any certainty. This leaves room for pleasing speculation about any piece which turns up with a mark difficult to account for. I have some spoons, late eighteenth century, which I believe came from Ireland; the only mark is GC, quite clear on the stem, and I like to think this is the mark of an unidentified silversmith who produced work with this mark in Belfast. On the other hand, it might just as well be the mark of George Cowles, London, who made spoons at that period; but then, with the strict supervision of the London guild, why should Cowles risk his mark on plate not otherwise hall-marked? As the value of such trifling articles is not in the least affected by their origin, the speculation is quite unprofitable, however amusing; but it illustrates a point about 'unascribed marks', and anyhow the spoons are very pretty.

10

The Hall-marking of Silver

THE LEOPARD'S HEAD

The earliest of all marks struck on silver by statute is the leopard's head. It is always so named, although to every appearance it is a lion's head. The reason is the peculiar language of heraldry at all times and particularly in its infancy. The statute of 1300 is in Norman-French, and specifies *une teste de leopart*. At that time in heraldry only a lion rampant was a lion, and in any other position it was a *lionne leopart*; modern heraldry has given up the leopard altogether and instead distinguishes many different attitudes of the lion. Thus the 'leopard' is in fact one of the three lions passant guardant of the Royal Arms, only the head being shown.

The statute of 1300 put upon the Wardens of the Company the duty of seeing that no silver was worked below standard, and having satisfied themselves, to 'touch' it with the leopard's head. It has been used ever since, except during the period 1697 to 1720. In the provinces, York adopted a mark of half of his head and a half fleur-de-lis conjoined. The earliest marks still extant show a large, handsome head, with a ducal crown (for Normandy), and with variations this continues up to 1697, even during the Commonwealth. On the resumption of this mark in 1720 it was mandatory throughout England, but is generally much smaller, although sometimes old stamps were used. From 1757 to 1820 it regained fair proportions and is much the best mark of the set. In 1821 a smaller shield was introduced and the crown removed, since when it has much more resembled an alley cat than a Royal Beast, in spite of occasional attempts to do something about its whiskers. The leopard's head, in similar form to the London one, was used by York until the closing of the office there, by Exeter until about 1780, by Newcastle until the office closed in 1884, by Chester until 1838, but never by Birmingham or Sheffield.

Because of its having been dropped by the other guilds, the leopard's head is often regarded as being the town mark of London, but it is, in fact, a Royal mark granted out of the Royal Arms. The shape of the shield, the size and general aspect of the leopard's head are of great value in determining a date when the other marks are obscure or uncertain; for example, it would be practically impossible to distinguish the hall-marks for London 1787 to 1795 from those for 1827 to 1835, were it not that in the former series the leopard is crowned and in the latter it is not. It is fair enough to say that the discrowning of the leopard marks the date at which the collector begins to lose interest.

The leopard's head was never used in Scotland or Ireland.

THE LION PASSANT

There is a certain amount of mystery about the lion passant, which was apparently adopted in 1544-5. No plate has been found before that date having this mark, and none is found afterwards without it; and yet there is no statute, no order of the Crown, no minute of the Company, or at least none now extant, which imposes it. The most probable explanation is that because previously the standard of the coinage had been strictly maintained the plate workers were enjoined that their standard must be 'no worse than the sterling'; but in 1542 Henry VIII debased the currency, again in 1544, and again in 1545, when it was only 4 of silver

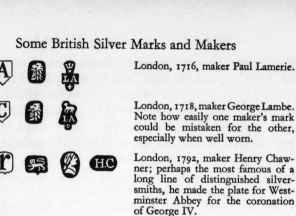

London, 1716, maker Paul Lamerie.

London, 1718, maker George Lambe. Note how easily one maker's mark could be mistaken for the other, especially when well worn.

London, 1792, maker Henry Chawner; perhaps the most famous of a long line of distinguished silversmiths, he made the plate for Westminster Abbey for the coronation of George IV.

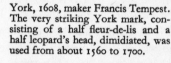

York, 1608, maker Francis Tempest. The very striking York mark, consisting of a half fleur-de-lis and a half leopard's head, dimidiated, was used from about 1560 to 1700.

Norwich, 1689, maker Thomas Haver; probably the last silversmith in the town, except perhaps James Daniel. Haver was Mayor in 1708, but the guild expired before 1700.

Exeter, probably between 1640 and 1650, possibly as late as 1680. Exeter plate of this period is rare, mostly spoons.

Exeter, 1817, maker Joseph Hicks. There were about half a dozen silversmiths in Exeter at this time, but the office also assayed for workers in Dartmouth and Plymouth. The guild died out in the middle of the nineteenth century.

Newcastle, 1790, makers Pinkney & Scott. The 'three castles' mark dates from about 1670. The guild was very active about 1800 but very little is found after 1820. Office discontinued 1884.

Chester, 1879, maker Joseph Knight, of Birmingham. By this period most of the silver assayed at Chester was made in Liverpool, Manchester or Birmingham.

Birmingham, 1798, maker Matthew Boulton, who made everything from pinchbeck buttons to steam engines. Boulton was the principal mover in having assay offices established in Sheffield and Birmingham.

Sheffield, 1816, maker John Law. Neither the Sheffield nor the Birmingham marks have varied very much since the offices were established in 1774. Sometimes, in small items, the crown is in the same shield with the date letter.

Edinburgh, 1642, maker Patrick Borthwick, deacon John Fraser. From communion plate, date ascertained from Kirk Session minutes.

Edinburgh, 1808, maker J. McKay. From a piece in the author's collection, formerly owned by Sir Walter Scott.

Glasgow, 1820, makers R. Gray & Son. One of the earliest examples with the lion rampant. The town mark, from the Burgh Arms, is probably the most elaborate ever struck. Used from about 1680.

Dublin, 1720, maker John Hamilton, one of the many Scotsmen who worked in Dublin. Early Dublin plate was worked to the highest standards and is much sought for.

Dublin, 1809, maker Joseph Johnson. The figure of Hibernia was introduced in 1747 to indicate that the (Irish) duty had been paid. After the Union in 1807 the Sovereign's head was stamped to show that United Kingdom duty had been paid, but Hibernia remains.

Cork, probably between 1770 and 1800, maker Joseph Nicolson. The only assay office in Ireland was in Dublin and by accepting such a mark the customer saved a risky journey and avoided the duty.

to 8 of alloy. At the same time the standard of silver remained the same when in the form of plate, and it seems reasonable that the Wardens should have agreed to put an additional stamp on all plate to show that it was not made from the debased coinage. The coinage became even worse, 3 of silver to 9 of alloy in 1551, and it was not until 1560, with Elizabeth I on the throne, that the old sterling was restored. The first documentary mention of the lion passant is in 1597, when two erring silversmiths were put in the pillory for counterfeiting marks on inferior plate, including 'the marks of Her Majesty's lion, the leopard's head, limited by statute, and the alphabetical mark'.

It is certainly remarkable that during the long period since 1300, when the coinage underwent debasement from time to time and eventually complete replacement by a base metal, that wrought plate should at all times have rigidly maintained its standard of purity. Perhaps a Company of traders is a better upholder of ethical standards than a Government!

In 1720 the lion passant was enacted for all plate wrought in England, and from that date it appears on the marks of all towns except those in Scotland or Ireland. In early London plate the lion passant shows considerable variation, but after 1720 the changes are minute, mainly in the details of the shape of the shield, and are not of great help in establishing a date, although it is serviceable in certain cases.

THE MAKER'S MARK

It is plain that from the earliest time it was usual for the maker to strike his mark on his work, and the omission might mean that the silver was sub-standard; but it became statutory only in 1363. From that date every smith had to have a mark 'known to the Wardens' which he must strike on his work *after* it had been assayed and 'touched with the leopard's head'. Unfortunately, however well these marks were known to the Wardens, they are all but unknown to us. It was usual to strike a sign or symbol, which might very well be the same as the sign above the shop; but there is no record of the association of the sign with any name. Later, it became common to use initials instead of or along with a symbol, but the large number of workers makes it very difficult to identify any pair of initials. There are not a dozen silversmiths whose marks can be positively identified before 1697, from which date all marks are clearly registered at Goldsmith's Hall. In Edinburgh, on the other hand, makers may be identified from about 1550, and in Dublin from about 1635.

The Act of 1697 raised the standard of silver and ordered the registration of marks, which must consist of the first two letters of the worker's surname, with an additional symbol at his pleasure. In 1720 the old standard was re-established and the workers had to mark with the ordinary initials of their Christian name and surname. This caused some confusion and in 1739 makers were ordered to destroy all old stamps and register new ones, which had to be the ordinary initials in a different letter from that previously used. Since that date the maker has been left alone by the legislature, at least so far as his own mark is concerned.

THE BRITANNIA MARK

In 1697 an Act decreed a higher standard of purity for wrought plate, and as well as altering the maker's marks it instituted a new mark altogether, a figure of Britannia and a lion's head erased. An Act of 1700 extended this mark to all provincial guilds. This was the only standard and mark permitted from 1697 to 1720, covering the period when London craftsmanship was at its highest point. Unfortunately, the Act of 1720 left it open to all to use the 'Britannia standard' and to mark it with the Britannia mark, and there are many instances of this being done, usually with pieces in imitation of the style of the period. Notes on this point are in Chapter 12.

Year				Year			
1658		𝕬		1678		𝖆	
1659	,,	𝕭	,,	1679	,,	𝖇	
1660	,,	𝕮	,,	1680		𝖈	
1661	,,	𝕯	,,	1681	,,	𝖉	,,
1662	,,	𝕰		1682	,,	𝖊	,,
1663	,,	𝕱	,,	1683	,,	𝖋	,,
1664	,,	𝕲	,,	1684	,,	𝖌	,,
1665	,,	𝕳	,,	1685	,,	𝖍	,,
1666	,,	𝕴	,,	1686	,,	𝖎	,,
1667	,,	𝕶	,,	1687	,,	𝖐	,,
1668		𝕷		1688	,,	𝖑	,,
1669	,,	𝕸	,,	1689		𝖒	
1670	,,	𝕹	,,	1690	,,	𝖓	,,
1671	,,	𝕺	,,	1691	,,	𝖔	,,
1672	,,	𝕻	,,	1692	,,	𝖕	,,
1673	,,	𝕼	,,	1693	,,	𝖖	,,
1674	,,	𝕽	,,	1694	,,	𝖗	,,
1675	,,	𝕾	,,	1695	,,	𝖘	,,
1676	,,	𝕿	,,	1696	,,	𝖙	,,
1677	,,	𝖀	,,				

to March 27th, 1697

1697, March 27th to May 29th

1697	,,		,,
1698	,,		,,
1699			
1700	,,		,,
1701	,,		,,
1702	,,		,,
1703	,,		,,
1704	,,		,,
1705	,,		,,
1706	,,		,,

1707	,,		,,
1708	,,		,,
1709	,,		,,
1710	,,		,,
1711	,,		,,
1712	,,		,,
1713	,,		,,
1714	,,		,,
1715	,,		,,

Notes)

The date-letter was changed annually, on the election of the new Court of Wardens, that is (since 1660), 29th May. Thus the date-letter given here as, for example, 1675, would in fact be struck up to the end of May 1676, and so for all other years.

Silver prior to the Restoration is very rare and its identification is not a matter for the amateur collector, earlier marks, therefore are not given.

The Court-hand letters for the cycle 1697 to 1715 are frequently very difficult to decipher when worn, but every collector should try to become familiar with them; the period represents the summit of what is generally available even to the wealthy collector.

Year		Letter		Year		Letter	
1716		A		1736		a	
1717	,,	B	,,	1737	,,	b	,,
1718	,,	C	,,	1738	,,	c	,,
1719		D		1739	,,	d	,,
1720	,,	E	,,	1740		d	
1721		F		1740	,,	e	,,
1722	,,	G	,,	1741	,,	f	,,
1723	,,	H	,,	1742	,,	g	,,
1724		I		1743	,,	h	,,
1725	,,	K	,,	1744	,,	i	,,
1726		L		1745	,,	k	,,
1727	,,	M	,,	1746	,,	l	,,
1728	,,	N	,,	1747	,,	m	,,
1729		O		1748	,,	n	,,
1730	,,	P	,,	1749	,,	o	,,
1731	,,	Q	,,	1750	,,	p	,,
1732	,,	R	,,	1751		q	
1733	,,	S	,,	1752	,,	r	,,
1734	,,	T	,,	1753	,,	ſ	,,
1735	,,	V	,,	1754	,,	t	,,
				1755	,,	u	,,

1756	🛡️	𝕬	🦁	1766	,,	𝕷	,,
1757	,,	𝕭	,,	1767	,,	𝕸	,,
1758	,,	𝕮	,,	1768	,,	𝕹	,,
1759	,,	𝕯	,,	1769	,,	𝕺	,,
1760	,,	𝕰	,,	1770	,,	𝕻	,,
1761	,,	𝕱	,,	1771	,,	𝕼	,,
1762	,,	𝕲	,,	1772	,,	𝕽	,,
1763	,,	𝕳	,,	1773	,,	𝕾	,,
1764	,,	𝕴	,,	1774	,,	𝕿	,,
1765	,,	𝕶	,,	1775	,,	𝖀	,,

Notes:

It should be noted that the use of the Britannia and lion's head marks were used for this standard of silver at any time after the sterling standard was re-enacted.

Many variations in the Leopard's Head and in the Lion Passant are to be found in the period 1720 to 1755.

Note the change in the shield of the date-letter in 1739–40.

Marks for the cycle 1756 to 1775 have sometimes been mistaken for those of the much earlier and rarer cycles 1658 to 1696. The shield of the lion passant, and the size and boldness of the leopard's head, are usually conclusive; also, the earlier marks are usually struck in some quite conspicuous place, the later ones usually under the base.

1776	🛡️	ⓐ	🦁		1796	👑	Ⓐ	🦁	👤
1777	,,	ⓑ	,,		1797	,,	Ⓑ	,,	,,
1778	,,	ⓒ	,,		1798	,,	Ⓒ	,,	,,
1779	,,	ⓓ	,,		1799	,,	Ⓓ	,,	,,
1780	,,	ⓔ	,,		1800	,,	Ⓔ	,,	,,
1781	,,	ⓕ	,,		1801	,,	Ⓕ	,,	,,
1782	,,	ⓖ	,,		1802	,,	Ⓖ	,,	,,
1783	,,	ⓗ	,,		1803	,,	Ⓗ	,,	,,
1784	,,	ⓘ	,,	👤	1804	,,	Ⓘ	,,	,,
1785	,,	ⓚ	,,	,,	1805	,,	Ⓚ	,,	,,
1786	,,	ⓛ	,,	👤	1806	,,	Ⓛ	,,	,,
1787	,,	ⓜ	,,	,,	1807	,,	Ⓜ	,,	,,
1788	,,	ⓝ	,,	,,	1808	,,	Ⓝ	,,	,,
1789	,,	ⓞ	,,	,,	1809	,,	Ⓞ	,,	,,
1790	,,	ⓟ	,,	,,	1810	,,	Ⓟ	,,	,,
1791	,,	ⓠ	,,	,,	1811	,,	Ⓠ	,,	,,
1792	,,	ⓡ	,,	,,	1812	,,	Ⓡ	,,	,,
1793	,,	ⓢ	,,	,,	1813	,,	Ⓢ	,,	,,
1794	,,	ⓣ	,,	,,	1814	,,	Ⓣ	,,	,,
1795	,,	ⓤ	,,	,,	1815	,,	Ⓤ	,,	,,

1816	🦁	Ⓐ	🦁	👤	1826	„	Ⓛ	„	„
1817	„	Ⓑ	„	„	1827	„	Ⓜ	„	„
1818	„	Ⓒ	„	„	1828	„	Ⓝ	„	„
1819	„	Ⓓ	„	„	1829	„	Ⓞ	„	„
1820	„	Ⓔ	„	👤	1830	„	Ⓟ	„	„
1821	🦁	Ⓕ	🦁	„	1831	„	Ⓠ	„	👤
1822	„	Ⓖ	„	„	1832	„	Ⓡ	„	„
1823	„	Ⓗ	„	„	1833	„	Ⓢ	„	„
1824	„	Ⓘ	„	„	1834	„	Ⓣ	„	„
1825	„	Ⓚ	„	„	1835	„	Ⓤ	„	„

Notes:

The period 1776 to 1780 is difficult to distinguish from the period 1736 to 1740, especially when worn. The shield of the lion passant should be carefully considered.

1784: the Sovereign's head stamped to show that plate duty had been paid. For the first two years the head is incuse, looking to the left; afterwards it is in cameo, looking to the right, not changing direction with succeeding sovereigns, as in the coinage, until the accession of Victoria.

1821: Leopard dis-crowned. Otherwise it would be difficult to distinguish, for example, 1827 from 1787.

F

1836				1856			
1837	,,	B	,,	1857	,,	b	,,	,,
1838	,,	C	,,	,,	1858	,,	c	,,	,,
1839	,,	D	,,	,,	1859	,,	d	,,	,,
1840	,,	E	,,	,,	1860	,,	e	,,	,,
1841	,,	F	,,	,,	1861	,,	f	,,	,,
1842	,,	G	,,	,,	1862	,,	g	,,	,,
1843	,,	H	,,	,,	1863	,,	h	,,	,,
1844	,,	I	,,	,,	1864	,,	i	,,	,,
1845	,,	K	,,	,,	1865	,,	k	,,	,,
1846	,,	L	,,	,,	1866	,,	l	,,	,,
1847	,,	M	,,	,,	1867	,,	m	,,	,,
1848	,,	N	,,	,,	1868	,,	n	,,	,,
1849	,,	O	,,	,,	1869	,,	o	,,	,,
1850	,,	P	,,	,,	1870	,,	p	,,	,,
1851	,,	Q	,,	,,	1871	,,	q	,,	,,
1852	,,	R	,,	,,	1872	,,	r	,,	,,
1853	,,	S	,,	,,	1873	,,	s	,,	,,
1854	,,	T	,,	,,	1874	,,	t	,,	,,
1855	,,	U	,,	,,	1875	,,	u	,,	,,

1876	🦁Ⓐ🦁👑			1886	,,	Ⓛ	,,	,,
1877	,,	Ⓑ	,,	,,	1887	,,	Ⓜ	,,	,,
1878	,,	Ⓒ	,,	,,	1888	,,	Ⓝ	,,	,,
1879	,,	Ⓓ	,,	,,	1889	,,	Ⓞ	,,	,,
1880	,,	Ⓔ	,,	,,	1890	,,	Ⓟ	,,	,,
1881	,,	Ⓕ	,,	,,	1891	,,	Ⓠ	,,	
1882	,,	Ⓖ	,,	,,	1892	,,	Ⓡ	,,	
1883	,,	Ⓗ	,,	,,	1893	,,	Ⓢ	,,	
1884	,,	Ⓘ	,,	,,	1894	,,	Ⓣ	,,	
1885	,,	Ⓚ	,,	,,	1895	,,	Ⓤ	,,	

Notes:

There are no difficulties throughout the whole of the Victorian period.

Note that the sovereign's head does not appear after 1890, the plate duty having been abolished.

1896		a		1916			a
1897	,,	b	,,	1917	,,	,,	b
1898	,,	c	,,	1918	,,	,,	c
1899	,,	d	,,	1919	,,	,,	d
1900	,,	e	,,	1920	,,	,,	e
1901	,,	f	,,	1921	,,	,,	f
1902	,,	g	,,	1922	,,	,,	g
1903	,,	h	,,	1923	,,	,,	h
1904	,,	i	,,	1924	,,	,,	i
1905	,,	k	,,	1925	,,	,,	k
1906	,,	l	,,	1926	,,	,,	l
1907	,,	m	,,	1927	,,	,,	m
1908	,,	n	,,	1928	,,	,,	n
1909	,,	o	,,	1929	,,	,,	o
1910	,,	p	,,	1930	,,	,,	p
1911	,,	q	,,	1931	,,	,,	q
1912	,,	r	,,	1932	,,	,,	r
1913	,,	s	,,	1933	,,	,,	s
1914	,,	t	,,	1934	,,	,,	t
1915	,,	u	,,	1935	,,	,,	u

1936	🦁	😺	**A**	1947	,,	,,	**M**
1937	,,	,,	**B**	1948	,,	,,	**N**
1938	,,	,,	**C**	1949	,,	,,	**O**
1939	,,	,,	**D**	1950	,,	,,	**P**
1940	,,	,,	**E**	1951	,,	,,	**Q**
1941	,,	,,	**F**	1952	,,	,,	**R**
1942	,,	,,	**G**	1953	,,	,,	**S**
1943	,,	,,	**H**	1954	🦁	😺	**T**
1944	,,	,,	**I**	1955	,,		**U**
1945	,,	,,	**K**	1956		🦁	😺	**a**
1946	,,	,,	**L**				

Notes:

In 1933 a 'Jubilee' mark was allowed, consisting of the heads of the then sovereign and consort; and in 1953 a 'Coronation' mark, featuring the crowned head of H.M. the Queen. These marks may be found on silver bearing the date letters for years both preceding and following those stated, and they are omitted as being of no service in establishing an exact date.

The marks are not always found in the order shown here. 1956 commences a new sequence with a new type of letter.

THE DATE-LETTER

An alphabetical system of marking the date of assay of each piece was adopted for London by statute in 1478 and has been carried on ever since, being adopted sooner or later by all other towns. In London the cycle is one of twenty letters, i and j being treated as one, v and u as one, and x, y and z omitted. The other guilds vary in their cycles, mostly using more letters. For some unexplained reason Sheffield, which began marking in 1773, has no order whatsoever in its date-letter until 1824, when a regular cycle commenced. The date-letters used in the various towns bear no relationship to each other.

The date-letter is the handiest way of identifying the year of the piece, and generally its form and the shape of the shield will tell all; but there are several London cycles which are very similar and one has to consider the presence or absence of the 'King's Head' or the leopard's crown to identify the cycle. Establishing the maker will generally close all doubt.

THE TOWN MARK

Each assay office has its own identifying mark. All English offices use as a general mark the lion passant. London uses the Royal mark of the leopard's head. Of the offices still in existence, Chester has the three wheat-sheafs and sword, Birmingham the anchor, and Sheffield the crown. In Scotland, Edinburgh has the castle and the thistle, Glasgow the laden tree and the figure of Caledonia. Dublin has the crowned harp and the figure of Hibernia. These are the marks at present in use, but earlier marks vary considerably and there are many towns which formerly marked but do so no longer. It is essential for the collector to study the town marks so that he may instantly recognize the assay office; without this knowledge he will find it a very difficult task to date any piece except a London one, as all the exhaustive indices of marks are grouped according to towns.

THE DUTY MARK, 'KING'S HEAD'

In 1784 a duty was imposed on all silver, and it was ordained that the representation of the head of the sovereign should be stamped on all plate to show that it had paid the duty. This was continued until 1890, when the duty was dropped. Certain very tiny articles were exempted from duty, but otherwise every piece of silver of this period has this mark. Like the 'crown or no crown' of the leopard's head, it is a very valuable aid when date-letters resemble each other closely. For example, the marks for 1816 to 1820 are almost identical with those for 1776 to 1780; but the former has the 'King's Head' and the latter has not.

In the first two years, 1784 and 1785, the incuse head of George III faces left and appears to be mistakenly punched, but it appears thus in all towns. Thereafter it is in cameo, facing the right for all sovereigns until the succession of Queen Victoria, when it faces left. It is not easy to distinguish one king from another, nor is this usually necessary, but by careful observation it can be done, occasionally useful when the date-letter is worn. Generally the mere presence or absence of this mark, together with the crown of the leopard, instantly identifies the cycle of date-letters.

The study of hall-marks is intensely interesting and several large and comprehensive works have been written on it. It is not, however, the chief end of the collector. It must be his aim to acquire such an intimate knowledge of the styles of the various periods, towns and workers that he can form a sound opinion about the provenance of any piece before he looks at the hall-mark. There are many desirable pieces where the hall-mark is quite illegible or worn completely out of existence, and it is then that real knowledge is indispensable. Do not base your opinion on the hall-mark; use it to confirm your opinion.

11

Sheffield Plate

THOMAS BOULSOVER, a Sheffield cutler, invented the process which became called Sheffield Plate about 1740, or possibly 1742. The date is uncertain, because no patent was taken out, and the operation was veiled in secrecy for a considerable time; but, of course, no technique which requires operatives will remain secret for long. The next known manufacturer was Joseph Hancock, in 1755, who marked his wares boldly with his name and town; but others also began, who made their marks to look as much as possible like the hall-marks of silver. Hence the savage Act of Parliament of 1757–8, which made bogus hall-marking a felony punishable by death. I am not aware of any executions under this Act. In 1773 an Assay Office was established in Sheffield, and any form of marking on Sheffield Plate became illegal. In 1784 the Sheffield Plate makers obtained an Act of Parliament legalizing a mark consisting of the full name of the maker and an associated device, and also enacting that any maker of goods plated with silver or resembling silver, operating within a hundred miles of Sheffield and desiring to place a mark on such wares, had to register the mark at the Assay Office of Sheffield. Sixteen makers registered that year. In all about 150 makers registered their marks between 1784 and 1840, when the process quickly died out against the competition of electro-plating.

The manufacture of Sheffield Plate is an interesting and

ingenious process, based on a thorough understanding of
the metals and using the fact that silver melts (954°C.) at a
slightly lower temperature than copper (1054°C.). An ingot
of copper is prepared, usually about an inch thick, two and
a half inches wide and ten inches long and weighing ten to
twelve pounds. A plate of ordinary standard silver is made
of the same length and breadth and about one-eighth of an
inch thick, weighing ten to twelve ounces; an ounce of
silver to a pound of copper represents a heavy plating.
When both sides are plated, as is more usual, each side has
about three-quarters of that weight, so that fair two-side
plating has about an ounce and a half of silver to each
pound of copper.

Both the silver and the copper are planed off absolutely
flat and true, and perfectly cleaned by potassium bichromate.
The least contamination, the touch of a finger, even a
breath, can spoil the whole process. The silver plates are
then placed on either side of the copper ingot and brought
into perfect optical contact, either by rolling or by hammering. The outside of the silver plates is then dusted with
French chalk and a copper plate, of about the same thickness as the silver, placed on each. The whole assembly is then
tied up with wire, twisted tightly. This assembly is now
placed in a furnace, which has a peephole in the door.
Through this the operator watches the ingot and immediately the silver commences to melt ('weep' was the
expressive technical term), the assembly is removed from the
furnace and allowed to cool. After removing the protective
outer copper plates, the silver is found to be completely
fused to the copper ingot and henceforth it can be treated as
a homogenous metal. It can be rolled out as thin as may be
desired, beaten and shaped. The silver will always retain
its proportion to the copper, and remains on the surface.
It is worked in exactly the same way as solid silver. Sheffield
Plate is therefore essentially different from electro-plating,

in which the article is completely fabricated in the base metal and then given a thin coating of pure silver.

A characteristic of Sheffield Plate is that the thickness of the plating is exactly proportioned to the thickness overall, so that when beaten out to one hundredth of an inch, about the average for the smaller shaped wares, the thickness of the silver is about one thousandth of an inch, comparable to good quality electro-plating; but in the case of trays and similar larger pieces these thicknesses are multiplied by three, which does not apply to the silver deposit in electro-plating. It follows, therefore, that the larger the article the thicker the silver; and it is thicker still when plated on one side only, the other side usually being tinned.

It is obvious that when Sheffield Plate is beaten out into shapes involving projections or chasing, the surface silver is subjected to stresses and the projection will receive much more friction than flat surfaces; sooner or later, the copper is going to show through. This is known as 'bleeding', and the piece thus worn is described as being 'bled'. It is important that in every description of bled plate the degree of bleeding should be stated as accurately as possible, 'bled on corners', 'bled on foliated border', 'bled all over'. The last term would denote that even on the plain surfaces the copper is showing, and the piece must therefore be regarded as worthless unless for some particular reason it is wanted for a specialist collection. A little bleeding on edges or decoration is not regarded as a serious defect in old Sheffield Plate; there is no pretence that it is solid silver and the bleeding shows that it is not electro-plate, which is seldom done on copper. In order to obviate or at least delay bleeding, it is not at all uncommon to find Sheffield Plate with edges of solid silver wire, or solid silver decorations. It was also common to insert a plate of solid silver, for example in the centre of a tray, to admit of a coat of arms or a presentation address being deeply engraved.

Sheffield Plate is considerably stronger than solid silver of the same dimensions, and this property was fully used. During its main period the candle was the only illuminant and large numbers of candlesticks were required in every family. These were made in great quantity in Sheffield Plate, from the simple bedroom candlestick with detachable holder, tray, thumb-handle and snuffer, to the most elaborate candelabra with numerous outstretched and curvilinear arms. In solid silver such pieces would require a great deal of metal, and the strength and cheapness of Sheffield Plate had a great advantage with all but the really wealthy. Similarly, this was the period when pierced work was at its highest popularity (a branch in which the English silversmith excelled all rivals) and the strength of Sheffield Plate admitted of very fine fretting without the thickening requisite in solid silver. In the Regency period not only cake-baskets of pierced designs but also great numbers of salts and mustards with blue glass liners were produced.

Sheffield Plate was frankly intended to simulate a more expensive article, and Sheffield never produced a school of artist-craftsmen. The fused plate was wrought by capable artisans, using mainly adaptations of the designs of the leading London silversmiths. There *were* original designs: when Flaxman was drawing his elegant classicisms for Wedgewood pottery, he was also designing for Fenton & Co., of Sheffield, from 1775 to 1787, and many of those designs have been identified. They do not display any extraordinary genius, tend to be rather over-ornamented and compare poorly with the ordinary commercial products of the period. The fact is that an artist, however distinguished in one field, is merely feeling his way when he designs for a medium in which he cannot personally operate.

It is probable that the smiths of Birmingham regarded with some envy the complete supremacy of their Sheffield brothers in this field. About 1806 a new development started in Birmingham, known as 'close plating'. It has been stated (but by a Sheffield man) that this was simply a revival of an old and well-known process, which may be the case; but I am not aware of any earlier examples. In this process, the article was fabricated and completed in iron; it was then dipped in tin and covered in silver leaf (one thousandth of an inch in thickness) and a hot polished iron run over it. This melted the tin (233 °C.) without melting the silver. It re-solidified almost immediately, very effectively soldering the silver to the iron fabrication. It was principally used for cutlery and similar articles, at that time called 'flat ware'. Experiment showed that it did not answer with larger pieces. One might have thought that with the presses then available it should have been possible to turn out such items as trays in large quantities using this process; but apparently not even the ingenuity of Birmingham could solve the associated problems and it remained mainly a cutlery process.

Birmingham being within a hundred miles of Sheffield, the Act of 1784 compelled the makers of close plate to register their marks there; and the quantities produced may be judged by the number of registrations. In the fifteen years up to 1805 eleven marks were registered; in the *ten* years following sixty marks were registered. It is difficult to be positive, and exceptions might be produced, but it would appear that Sheffield Plate was exclusively a Sheffield product and close plate exclusively a Birmingham one, both being produced concurrently over a period of about thirty-five years, all the Birmingham makers having to register their marks at Sheffield.

Sheffield Plate thus falls into clearly definable periods. In the first, from its invention about 1740 to 1772, it was not within the cognisance of the law, and manufacturers applied what marks pleased them. In this period the standards of workmanship are not generally very high. The second period is from 1773 to 1784, during which no marks of any kind could be applied. There was a considerable advance both in quality and in quantity at this time. Unfortunately one is left to one's own 'sense of period' and to define designers or makers is hazardous. In the third period, 1784 to 1840, makers register their marks and dates can be established within certain limits. During part of this period, from 1807 onwards, Birmingham makers of 'close plate' also registered their marks at Sheffield, but very little of their utilitarian production has survived. The earlier part of this period is the heyday of Sheffield Plate; after 1820, embellishment begins to become more important than design.

In 1840 Mr. Wright, a surgeon in Birmingham, took out a patent in conjunction with G. H. and H. Elkington for plating base metals with silver by an electrolytic process. This process allowed of the whole work being fabricated in the base metal and all errors corrected before being coated with silver of any desired thickness and perfectly even deposit. The commercial advantages of the process were overwhelming and in a very few years both close plating and Sheffield Plate were history. For a few years Sheffield Plate was used for the bodies of large articles such as urns, the smaller parts being electro-plated, but this was only a transitional stage until plating vats could be made large enough. So far as I can ascertain, all the silver-plated articles exhibited at the Great Exhibition of 1851 were electro-plated and it is fortunate that the earlier process died in time; one would not like to think of those horrors being perpetrated in the elegant and kindly Sheffield Plate.

12

Acquiring Silver

THERE ARE various methods of acquiring silver. The most favoured ancient method, armed robbery, is now discountenanced, and therefore I shall give no directions. The only method of acquiring silver without some monetary transaction is by inheritance, and even here the State, that most powerfully-armed robber, will no doubt demand tribute. It is worth paying. Nothing can form a better basis for a collection than inherited plate, especially if it bears the family crest or coat of arms. This it is your duty to preserve. Even if you don't like the style, there are bound to be some members of the family growing up who will expect a wedding present some time or other, and what better? Even the lengthy inscription, which reduces the value in the eyes of other collectors, enhances it in yours as solid testimony to the 'esteem and regard' in which at least one of your forbears was held by some of his contemporaries. Family silver should never be sold, unless upon some irresistible pressure.

Such pressures do, however, arise so that the collector finds himself with silver bearing coats of arms, crests or inscriptions which have nothing to do with him. The first fierce pride of possession inclines one to remove everything and substitute one's own, but this should be resisted. The more recent the silver, the less the harm. If you have a salver made in 1910 and bearing the arms of Smith of Smithsville,

by all means have your own put on instead, always suppos-
ing that your arms were granted before 1910. But probably,
as your collection and your taste develop, and after perusal
of American magazines, you will decide that this passion
for 'personalizing' is puerile, like buying a registration
number which happens to include your initials. Early silver
is by no means diminished by arms or crest. Nobody would
ever dream of obliterating the Royal Arms, and even the
finest piece by Paul Lamerie would be enhanced if it bore the
arms of Holles, Duke of Newcastle. So with lesser families.
The arms may not be known to you, but they will be known
to any student of heraldry. It always adds to the interest of
an old piece if it bears a *contemporary* coat or crest; if added
later it is usually a depreciation. Thus if you are having new
plate made, certainly have your coat, or crest, or mono-
gram; but if you are collecting old silver, best leave it alone.
The nearer the condition in which it left the silversmith's
workshop the better.

As inheritances are usually too small and too seldom,
you must purchase; and there are many ways in which you
can do so. The first, the best, the most expensive and the
least interesting, is to purchase from one of the great London
dealers—they don't like to call themselves dealers, almost
anything else, but not *dealers,* although obviously anybody
who buys an article and sells it again is a dealer; but I
distinguish them as *great* dealers. Anyway, here you have
nothing to worry about, except perhaps the bill. Do not,
however, expect to find a vast stock of the particular kind
of silver you are looking for, unless you are looking for
some heavily decorated mid-Victorian silver, in which case
you have tons to choose from. You may go into the greatest
dealer nowadays and ask for a nice Queen Anne or George I
coffee-pot, or a really pretty Regency cake-basket, and find
they have nothing to show you; but if you care to call in
early next week there will be a selection. The fact is that

such things are so scarce that the great dealers have generally an amicable arrangement; they all have a pretty good idea of what everybody else has in stock, and if one has a customer and another has the article, well, the great thing is to bring the two together and the margin is divided on well-understood lines. This is a perfectly honest and sound arrangement. You pay no more, and it means that the whole stocks of all the great dealers will be turned over to find what you want. One large department store, which has an antique silver department, prefers not to buy although they advertise; they like to make a register, so that if they have an inquiry they can look up the register and see if they have a selling client who has what is wanted. They claim that by this method they can give a more favourable price both to buyer and to seller, as they have not the expense of holding stock, but somehow I do not feel this is how a *great* dealer should operate.

Buying from a great dealer is like buying from any other really good shop. You are attended by well-mannered and knowledgeable people, you can be quite sure that the description is absolutely correct and if there is any error it will be put right; but you cannot expect bargains. The shop must carry its overheads, which are substantial, and you must expect to pay the full price for everything; after all, everything is being done for you.

The next method is by purchase from a small dealer, which covers quite a lot of people. Very few small dealers trade in silver alone and one can learn quite a few things about them from the other things they have. The man who also deals in clocks, watches and jewellery is usually expert in old silver also; sometimes he likes to parade his expertize, sometimes he would like to be thought ignorant. In the latter case, be wary. If you buy something which is not what you think it is, your principal claim against the seller is that you relied on his 'skill and knowledge'; but if he has al-

Above, cake-basket. An example of the pierced work in which English silversmiths of the period excelled. London 1767. Maker: W. Plummer. *Below*, George III entrée dish, one of a pair. The elegant proportions and sparse decoration are typical of the Regency. London 1812. Maker: William Taylor

Left, George I jug, 10½ ins. high, bearing the arms of Dartrey, Co. Monaghan. Irish silver of this period is justly prized. Dublin 1715. Maker: T. Williamson. *Below*, pair of wine coolers, 10½ ins. high, with eight wine coasters, four 6½ ins. in diameter and four 6 ins. They bear the arms of Coote. Unusually ornate for this period, the decoration is superbly handled. (J. W. Storey & Wm. Elliot)

ready disclaimed any skill and knowledge, you are not likely
to make good your claim. The dealer who has a varied stock
of hardware, china, pewter and small articles of furniture is
usually one who is not particularly expert in any one line
but has a good idea of what his customers want and what
they are willing to pay for it. Then there is the dealer who
buys very widely and is content with just so much margin
(sometimes surprisingly low) on everything, regardless of
what the potential value is. From both these last two types
it is possible to buy very well, but naturally the better you
know your silver the better you will buy. You will seldom
have any 'come-back' if you rue your bargain, and the advice
below on buying by auction applies here.

A knowledgeable small dealer can give you a better start
in collecting than anybody else. I was started off by a dealer
who was a most respected expert but kept a small shop in
a country village. He made me a present of a Chien-Lung
mug which had a little chip out of it, and sold me a very fine
Regency tea-pot for £12 10s. I was off, and his friendly
interest and disinterested advice were of the greatest service
to me in my salad days.

Private purchase is a favourite method of acquisition by
dealers, but I do not recommend it for the private collector.
The dealer advertises and on a reply calls on the seller. The
usual method is to group together a number of pieces, even
if only three, and make an offer for the lot. The reason for
this is that he does not wish to price each item separately,
to give a free valuation on which the seller may deal with
somebody else. The other method is to call on the seller to
name his price—'I can't be both buyer and seller'. The great
dealer advertises, but generally the seller takes or sends the
silver and receives a very fair offer. In my opinion, most of
the offers to buy or sell silver by private bargain are, in fact,
covert trade transactions. Sometimes a private seller has
tried the trade and been dissatisfied with the price offered,

G

in which case there is no harm in seeing what he has to sell; but let him name his price and either take it or leave it. Haggling is for the small dealers. Another risk of private purchase is that you may be buying stolen goods, which, if traced, you must give up without recompense. On the whole, I think that private purchase should be left to dealers. I have never done it.

The last method is the most interesting and probably most exciting method, full of pitfalls and hazards, but, for those who know what I have tried to impart, the best way of getting a collection together—public auction. Theoretically, this is perfect. Theoretically, everything is properly described in the catalogue, you have made a complete examination of the piece in which you are interested, and people bid only because they wish to acquire the piece. It does sometimes happen that all these theories work out in practice and you must do your best to ensure this.

The first thing to keep in mind is that your bid is your own. Nobody can make you bid if you don't want to bid. Therefore, if you bid too much it is because you are ignorant of the true value, or because the cupidity to possess has got the better of you, or vanity that you will not stop bidding once you have begun. Two of these are deadly sins, and the first is the deadliest of all in the auction room.

The second thing is that once you have bid you have bid, and only in the rarest circumstances may you retract; and if you do, it is quite open to the autioneer to debar you from ever bidding again in that saleroom. The whole principle of auctioneering depends on this: that the bidder will fully and promptly implement his bid. Nothing is more likely to get you the ill-will of the auctioneer and all his staff than quibbling about your bill, and once you have got their ill-will you will find that somehow nothing ever goes right for you again. Of course, this does not refer to genuine mistakes which every good auctioneer is anxious to put right as soon as possible. If, for example, you thought you were bidding for item 96, whereas in fact it was 95 that was put up, you must get up on your feet and declare it then and there; the auctioneer then *may*, in his own discretion, re-expose item 95. It is bad practice, however, for it is surprising how seldom a re-exposed item will fetch as much as 75 per cent of the highest former bid.

Disputes may, of course, arise, in spite of perfect good faith on all sides. I once attended a very good-class auction where a number of articles which had belonged to Sir Walter Scott had been sent in by descendents. There were a number of dessert forks and spoons, bearing the Scott crest. I was a little short of these at the time, as they are much scarcer than table forks and spoons in that period, and with the idea of a relic of the great Sir Walter thrown in, one way or another I bought them for about three times as much as a prudent person would have paid for the ordinary run of such silver. At home, looking up the hall-marks, I found they were for 1836, four years after Sir Walter's death, and ten years after he had presumably stopped buying silver. I wrote the auctioneers, who replied that both they and the vendors had described the items in good faith. The hammer was down, there was no come-back. This I just had to swallow as best I could; but I had bought a number of items at this sale, and by a curious coincidence the clerk had made an error, I think of £10, in adding up my account. The error was in my favour and when the auctioneers wrote to me to send the difference I replied with great glee that I had paid the sum demanded, the hammer was down, etc. I forget the exact terms on which the matter was finally adjusted, but I remember it finished with a whisky and hand-shake.

Moral: Look up the marks *before* you bid, and don't attach too much importance to extrinsic circumstances. Buy silver, never mind who *may* once have owned it.

Silver at auction is often sold at 'per ounce', except in the case of weighted articles such as candlesticks. Included are such as dressing-cases, where only the mounts are silver, and Indian or Chinese silver not hall-marked. In such cases no weight is given and the item is sold 'all at'.* When the non-silver element is trivial it is usual to make an allowance; a proper catalogue would state, 'Chocolate-pot, London, 1802, Hester Bateman, cocus-wood handle, 28½ oz. allow 1½, 27 oz.'. The tale is told of a lady who entered a saleroom while the auction was proceeding, was immediately attracted by a pretty Queen Anne tea-pot which was being held up, and entered the bidding. Ultimately it was knocked down to her at £18, on which her neighbour remarked 'Pretty stiff price.' She replied, 'I think it is a very nice little tea-pot for £18,' and promptly fainted when told she had bid more than £500.

It is important to remember that in the sale-room you are on your own. The auctioneers, for their own reputation, will make up the catalogue as accurately as they can, but you will always find on the first page a disclaimer of any responsibility. In especial, they are not required to draw attention to defects, although some do, or cover by adding 'w.a.f.', meaning 'with all faults'. As has already been shown, there is sometimes difficulty in dating, and it is natural to give the seller the advantage of the doubt. Check the hall-marks yourself. If you think the catalogue is wrong, discuss it with the auctioneer before the sale. Even if the marks are correct there is a further possibility, in the case of the more important pieces, that they may have been transposed. To do such a thing intentionally is, of course, a serious crime, but serious crimes are committed and if the transposing of marks had not become a serious matter it is unlikely that the Act of 1844 would have been so explicit. Not only is the

* It is becoming increasingly usual for silver to be sold under this condition.

transposing of marks to any other article, whether gold, silver or base metal, specified as a crime, but also cutting off marks, and affixing marks from other plate.

It might be supposed that it would be easier for the defrauder to use false dies for stamping, but this is not the case. Every skilled silversmith can cut out a mark and fix it into another piece, but working with steel is a very different matter and it is extremely difficult to counterfeit an old mark successfully. Moreover, the dies would have to be used quite often to make it worth while and suspicion would be aroused if important, unknown pieces with the same marks began to turn up. Then the possession of the dies would instantly prove guilt, whereas transplanting is very difficult to prove. In fact, I have never heard of a prosecution for this offence, but 'the trade' is sure that it has been done and possibly is still being done, perhaps more widely than might be supposed. Certainly the gains could be enormous.

In the case of any important piece, therefore, you will examine it carefully for the least trace of patching in the vicinity of the hall-marks. If you are suspicious, leave it alone. Don't start an argument. Something will turn up some other time.

The Britannia mark raises some difficulties for the inexperienced. This mark, denoting the higher standard of silver, was the only legal mark from 1697 to 1720, but since that time it has been open to any silversmith to use the higher standard and the Britannia mark, the only other identifying marks being the date-letter and the maker's mark; if these are more or less obliterated you might persuade yourself that you had a Queen Anne piece. This should not happen once you have a little experience. The size, the weight, the workmanship are different. The earlier marks are much larger and more boldly struck. Even in photographs one could easily distinguish between two 'porringers' of mine, one 1709 the other 1905, both with the

Britannia mark. I am quite sure these were never used for porridge, but for the purpose I use them for, to hold sugar.

In general, you should aim at attaining such a knowledge of your subject that the hall-marks are of secondary importance. You ought to be able to recognize at a glance the period and the quality. If these are what you want, bid for it. What does the exact date or the maker's name *really* matter? It is the silver you are buying. There were heroes before Agamemnon, and there were consummate silversmiths before Paul Lamerie. Fashions change in silver as well as everything else, and you would be unwise to pay a fancy price for a piece solely because it was by a currently fashionable maker. It is the design, the workmanship and the period that matter, although it is all to the good if the maker and date can be ascertained.

Very often silver sold by auction is in poor condition, and it is then that good judgement is rewarded. Generally, any amount of tarnishing is acceptable, but no corrosion. You will soon find it easy to distinguish between the smooth blue-black of tarnish and the slightly roughish grey of corrosion. Until you acquire enough experience you may carry a piece of Dura-glit impregnated cotton-wool in a plastic envelope and clean a tiny part of the tarnished plate —if it clears up, all is well; if not, it is corroded, and you do best by leaving it for the scrap-buyers.

The kind of damage you may accept is important. Dents or distortions can be corrected, large dents more easily than small deep ones. Cracks along the edge of a piece should be avoided; they are expensive to repair perfectly. Of course, if you are willing to take it into your collection, cracks and all, good and well; but as you progress you will not be happy with it. Sometimes one finds parts of decorative features worn into holes, as bar-and-bead on tray-edges or corners of candlesticks. In the former case, it may be possible to have the beading repaired or replaced, and this may be worth while if you buy it cheap enough; but where candle-sticks are worn into holes it is a sure sign that the whole job is far too light, concealed by the weight of the base. To repair would be far more expensive than the result would justify. Candlesticks should always be bought with care. They are popular and fetch good prices, but unless the bottom weight can be removed you really do not know how much silver you are buying. It is a good idea to balance it across the edge of the hand. The nearer the base the point of balance, the less the actual silver.

It is not at all a bad policy to buy silver which is heavily tarnished or needing easy repair. The dealers are much more likely to let you have such pieces. What they want to buy is stock they can put on their shelves immediately and sell at a profit. They don't want to tie up capital in a piece that is going to be three months in Birmingham before it can be made saleable. But in the case of really fine silver, before 1730 perhaps, it is better to go the price for something in good condition. Damage will greatly reduce its value, and repair will do so much more.

On viewing day, mark on your catalogue what you want to buy and the price you have decided to bid. Don't go for too much. Avoid opening the bidding. Let it go on until it shows signs of flagging at less than your marked price, then strike in. If it goes beyond your price before you even start, let it go. Never be the bidder who opens for almost every-thing, in the hope of a wonderful bargain, and drops out long before a reasonable price has been reached. Much better have it said of you, 'He doesn't bid often, but when he bids he buys'. Do not, however, make a fetish of this; once your price has been passed, drop out. If you *always* buy when you bid, you are very liable to find yourself being consistently 'run up' by some sportive dealer. When bidding, it is usual to do so by some gesture with your catalogue. At your first bid it may be necessary to call or otherwise draw the auctioneer's attention to yourself, but once you have bought something he will always give a glance to see if you are bidding. When you drop out of the bidding make this clear by shaking the head when the auctioneer looks towards you. Do this promptly, and never re-start. Don't look to see who else is bidding and never show any sign of pleasure or of disappointment.

By far the greatest part of all silver sold by auction is bought by dealers. Comparatively few amateurs have the knowledge, and the confidence to back that knowledge, which are essential for successful bidding. The dealer has, and the further advantage that dealers have usually a good understanding with each other; in other words, the ring. A ring may consist of two neighbours saying, 'I won't bid for the cakestand if you don't bid for the toastrack'; or a family saying 'We'll let Harry do all the bidding, he's good at it, and after the sale we'll sort things out'; or two dealers saying, 'Well, if you have a customer for the tea-pot, all right, but I'm short of cutlery'; or the full ring at a big sale, when, no matter who buys anything, it all goes into the pool and is auctioned again at a private meeting, perhaps in an hotel, perhaps in the premises of one of the members, when 'fair trade prices' are bid and the surplus is divided between everybody; for after all, the dealer who did not bid has contributed just as much to the pool as the one who did. Every one of these arrangements is illegal, specifically forbidden by the Auctions (Bidding Agreements) Act of 1927, a copy of which must be exhibited in every auction room or anywhere an auction is held. This is a well-meaning piece of legislation, the intention being that if you put anything up for sale by auction you will get the full market price, not kept down by private arrangements between buyers. Its only defect is that it provides no means whatever for enforcing it, and in my view it is impossible to do so: it would require at least two policemen to become accepted as dealers, to be accepted into the ring and to be present at all their dealings. I have never heard of a conviction under this Act, although every dealer, every auctioneer and every frequenter of auctions knows that the ring exists and quite often everybody who is in it. The sensible thing is to accept the fact that the Act is a dead letter and learn to live with the ring.

Or rings. At a large sale there may be several, the big boys who want Regency or earlier, the little boys who want Victorian or anything, and the gold and jewellery boys. They may overlap a little, but they generally manage to keep off each other's toes.

At first sight the existence of rings of dealers might seem to be not at all a bad thing for the private buyer. If they are not going to go beyond a very restricted figure the private bidder will have it all his own way beyond that, and he can very well afford to pay more than the trade wants to. Unfortunately it doesn't work out like that. The dealers all have stock on their shelves and they cannot allow its value to be depreciated by private buyers getting plate at auction at very much less prices. Therefore if a private buyer comes in it is in their interest to see that he pays as nearly as possible the full retail price. Time and again at auctions you will find that after the miscellaneous bidders have dropped out tnere are two left who carry the price on much further; in most cases it is a private buyer and the bidder for the ring, who does not want to purchase at that price but does not want it to go too cheaply into private hands. With that extra sense that constant attendance at auctions engenders, the trade bidder knows just how far he can push the rival, and if by chance the ring is the buyer, well, it goes into the common stock, a bad buy but well covered by the other purchases.

The remedy is in your own hands. All you have to do is to follow the advice I have already given. If you decide before-

hand what you are going to bid, nobody can force you to
go further and the ring will become chary of running you
up if they are being left with fairly pricey purchases. This
is where the friendly dealer already mentioned can be of
great assistance to you. If you tell him quite casually the
few things you are interested in, he may pass this information on and you will not be run up much beyond the trade
price; that is as long as you stick to what you have said and
don't go bidding for everything that comes up.

In many respects dealers form a strange fraternity,
differing widely in the scope of their operations but nevertheless preserving a sodality among themselves, no doubt
partly because a government has made illegal what they
consider to be a perfectly fair aspect of their trading arrangements. Consequently a large part of their business among
themselves is transacted by word of mouth, and I have
never heard of a dealer going back on his word. They extend
the same good faith to everybody, and you can be as sure
of a verbal bargain as you could be with a stockbroker or a
member of Lloyd's. Their interests in the saleroom are
opposed to yours yet it is possible to establish a vague sort
of live-and-let-live relationship with most of them; if you
can do so, it will be very much to your advantage.

13

Forming a General Collection

ONE OF the advantages of a collection of old silver is its fluidity. If you buy prudently you are never stuck with anything; you can turn it back into money immediately. You can graduate from a modest collection to something rich and rare. You will do best, however, if you start with some sort of plan in your mind, for at least the first few years of collecting.

To begin with you must acquire a knowledge of silver. This you can do from books to a certain extent, but in general the illustrations are of fine and rare pieces not likely to come your way in the ordinary course. Nothing can take the place of seeing and handling silver, and fortunately it is easy to get this practical education. There are in London several large warehouses of miscellaneous silver where you are welcome to wander round at your leisure; thus you will learn the normal retail prices at the time. Visit auctions. Spend a lot of time on the view day examining the pieces and make notes on your catalogue. Go to the sale, don't buy, but note the prices. Visit the smaller dealers, see their stocks, chat with them. If you find one whom you like and if something strikes your fancy, say a dozen Regency teaspoons, make a purchase from him; thus you are established as a buyer, not a mere lounger passing the time—it is surprising how much of a dealer's time is taken up by such people.

Most people nowadays collect silver which is of practical use. The merely ornamental, like the Victorian table centre-piece, is not wanted, and if you like you can buy that sort of thing very cheaply; but you might have difficulty in selling it at all, cheap or dear. The best thing to start with is cutlery, and I recommend the simplest type of Queen's pattern early Victorian. The late Georgian fiddle pattern is not particularly pretty and the earlier Old English forks are usually too worn to be really serviceable, while the spoons are perhaps too light and too expensive for every-day use. Then some salts and peppers, and here you might launch out a little and get half-a-dozen Regency salts, circular on three feet, as plain as possible, and cylindrical peppers. All these you must use at every meal, so that you become absolutely familiar with the feel of silver.

Still keeping to the table, the next thing would be sauce-boats, preferably in a set of four, but exact matching is not a necessity. These should be on three feet, of good size and weight; Regency period is to be preferred, but one may find excellent reproductions made in Birmingham (and often marked in Chester) between 1900 and 1914. These are often too small and too light, and tend to decoration, but they can be found of a size, weight and simplicity to make very satis-factory temporary substitutes for Georgian. Then one must have a pair of candlesticks, and to keep down costs these may very well be in Sheffield Plate; but let them be small, preferably 9 or 10 inches high, certainly not more than a foot, with two branches as simple as possible.

Next, one must think of the tea-table, and the first requisite is a Regency tea-pot, between 1810 and 1820, boat-shaped, preferably with a silver handle having ivory heat-insulating inserts. This will be very plain, but with a single band of exquisitely fine engraving, and the lid will be beautifully shaped with a silver rectangular knob. Do not in this case content yourself with an early twentieth-century reproduction, not at all the spirit of the original. You must have a sugar-bowl and cream-jug, not necessarily to match but in the same spirit; I have always used a Queen Anne or similar two-handled 'porringer' for sugar, and there is no harm in using a small sauce-boat for cream, although a taller jug is less liable to spill. If you are one of those who believe in pouring hot water on exhausted tea-leaves, you may want a hot-water jug, or even a kettle on a stand with a spirit-flame underneath. How little these are used nowadays may be judged by how very cheaply you can buy them. I once had three spirit-kettles and I cannot remember ever seeing one used. Better use an electric kettle, and get a really good Regency cake-basket, very similar to the tea-pot. Pierced-work cake-baskets can be very hand-some, my personal preference is for plain. Some people use these also for fruit, but there is a danger of fruit juices causing quite difficult stains on the basket; a little piece of transparent plastic cut to shape will obviate any risk and be invisible.

Now for coffee. We have to face the fact that once the bug has bitten, you will never be quite happy until you have a Queen Anne or early Georgian coffee-pot, which will cost you money you ought not to expend until you have gained a lot of experience. You ought to buy one of those Early Victorian pear-shaped pots—they were used either for tea or coffee—that can be found quite pleasing if not elegant in shape, with hot-milk jugs similar and not too expensive. The coffee-pots of the Classical periods, 1760–80, 1795–1820, do not fit in with the sort of nucleus collection I have in mind, besides costing a great deal more money.

A salver should now be sought, as plain as possible, although a crest or coat of arms is not a blemish. It should be of good weight for its size, and I have a strong preference for a Dublin salver of the Regency period. You may have to pay a little more for it, but it is a sound investment. Earlier salvers (or waiters as they are often called) come much more expensive as one goes further back into the eighteenth century. There is always a demand. Everybody wants a good salver, and can always use more, so you must expect to pay a good deal more per ounce than you would for, say, a two-handled standing cup of the same date.

The next thing to look for is a pair of wine coolers, and these may very well be in Sheffield Plate. Here one does not want them *too* plain, a gadroon edge and a fluted body improve the appearance of these comparatively large vessels. There is nothing wrong with having a single wine cooler, which will cost less than half of a pair, but the chances of matching it up later are very small indeed. You may very well buy a single one, with the intention of disposing of it when a good pair turns up; whether you are allowed to do so will depend on other circumstances, for whether or not you like to cool your wine on the sideboard, a wine cooler sets off wonderfully the art of the flower arranger.

All that remains is to complete your table appointments. While a cruet-stand is far from necessary under modern conditions, it can be a very handsome addition to the table. I prefer the pierced work of the 1770–90 period, and these can be bought very reasonably, if you wait and look around; much less per ounce than a salver of the same period, possibly less than half, and the bottles thrown in. It is well to have a good look at a cruet, to satisfy yourself that each detachable part is hall-marked with the same mark, and also that all the tops have also the same mark. The bottles should match and be original. Of course, you may very well accept a replacement top or an odd bottle, but you will expect to pay less, and if you want to sell it you must not be too avaricious, whereas if you have acquired a perfect original set you can take it into any big dealer and walk out with a satisfying cheque in exchange.

A sugar-dredger, preferably a pair, should be acquired.

Here I advise the early twentieth-century reproductions of the Queen Anne style. There are some very fine 'tapered-cylinder' dredgers of the later Georges and these are excellent if you do not intend to go earlier eventually; but in all probability you will want a 'Britannia' dredger sooner or later, and meanwhile the reproduction will do very well.

Silver entrée dishes are perhaps not so essential nowadays, when many sets of table china include them; but although china keeps its heat it is, of course, vulnerable to impact or oven heat. Since they are not now so popular, entrée dishes are not too expensive, and you can purchase a Regency piece for perhaps one-third of the price per ounce you would have to pay for a cake-basket of the same period; or you may have them in Sheffield Plate for very little money. As recently as 1964 I saw a fine set of four oblong dishes with covers, in perfect condition and of a desirable size, sold by auction for £20. The oblong shape is to be preferred to the oval; you can put four oblong dishes on an ordinary electric hot-plate which will accommodate only two ovals. Get a set of four, even if you have to wait a while; odds will only irritate you. If you are buying silver ones, look at each piece carefully. It is not at all uncommon to find a handsome Regency cover on a Sheffield Plate dish; reasonable enough at the time when the only way to keep it warm was to set a candle under it, but in such a case it is only a Regency dish-cover you are buying, not worth much more than the ordinary run of good recent silver.

Now you have, for the cost of a very small motor-car, an excellent 'downsitting' of silver, and you may eat your dinner or entertain your guests 'with all things mighty rich and handsome' about you . You are not yet a collector; but you have the essentials of a collection. Where you go from here depends largely on how much money you are willing to invest in silver, always remembering that what is bought with reasonable prudence can always be put back into as much or more money. Always buy what is of some real use under modern social conditions. A jug can be used for hot or cold water, or for cocktails, for milk or for coffee; but a two-handled standing cup of the 'trophy' variety is of very little use except perhaps as a flower vase. You will find that the jug may cost you twice as much per ounce as the cup, but it is the better purchase.

You must now develop in a chosen direction, for example expanding and improving the Regency part of your collection. I have already suggested that if one is collecting for posterity the 'Art Noveau' of the period 1890 to 1914 offers a possibility; it can be bought for little more than the melting-down price, but it is a fair prophecy that before 2050 it will be eagerly and expensively sought for. However, as you were going to remark, what has posterity done for you? As far as this generation is concerned, the Regency period is the best to collect. There is a lot of it about, it is extremely elegant, and it can be bought at reasonable prices, less than new silver. The mid-eighteenth-century silver is much more expensive and not really any better; if you are able to spend folding money it is better to go right to the beginning of the century and get a coffee service of the 'Britannia' period.

Sooner or later the question of silver plates will come up, and here it is time to pause and consider. Silver is not the ideal material for plates: it cools rapidly and knives make deep scores on the surface. And you cannot collect them as you go along, you have to go for a complete matched set, which will cost a lot of money. It really depends on the kind of household you maintain; if you run to a butler and a couple of footmen, nothing can be more suitable, nothing can look so well, as silver plates all round; but for a more modest establishment, there is a lot to be said for china. A few silver plates as canapé-trays do very well, and if you buy an odd lot of say five or nine you will buy considerably cheaper than matched dozens.

George III: *right*, a pair of candlesticks. They are more or less Adam style, but lack the severe elegance of London. Sheffield 1788. Maker: John Parsons & Co. *Below*, dinner plate, one of a dozen, 10½ ins. in diameter. Bears the arms of Onslow

Above, heavily-tarnished silver, after years in storage. The veining is beginning to close up and it will soon be black all over. By modern methods, however, all its former brilliance can be quickly and easily restored. *Below*, silver in use. Except for rare or delicate pieces, silver should be kept in daily use.

In general you should avoid very large pieces, over 100 ounces; however cheaply you may buy them, you may find it difficult to translate them back into money again. Never buy on an impulse—you will invariably regret it. Don't buy something in the hopes that you will find a use for it—you won't. Define to yourself what your requirements are, and then go out and see what you can find. Patience is essential. When you have been round enough warehouses, and attended enough auction sales, you will know that something will always turn up sooner or later. At the same time you must never miss a chance when it offers, as long as you are sure of your ground; as English silver continues to flow across the Atlantic, the chances become fewer, and you must take them when you may.

H

14

The Specialist collection

THE SPECIALIZED collection is quite different from a general collection, although that must be its beginning. Nobody can set out to make a special collection unless he has a general collection already. You need quite a lot of experience before you can even make up your mind in what direction you want to specialize. You must have handled and seen and bought a great deal of silver; then you may find you have a definite preference, or you may quite deliberately decide that there is an area not overworked which you would like to develop. There are fashions in collecting as well as anything else and it is quite possible for one man to start a fashion; all you have to do is collect enough of anything then write about your collection, or get somebody else to do so. Take, for example, the current passion for Carl Fabergé. For ten years after his death in 1920 dealers were actually breaking up some of his work for the small value of the gold. For a ten-pound note you could buy a gold and enamel cigarette-case which would cost you a thousand pounds forty years later, and today you must have earned your first million a long time ago before you may aspire to own one of his Easter eggs. Anybody who laid out a few thousand pounds in 1925 on Fabergé would have a collection worth a million today. Yet this extraordinary surge of fashion was the work of one man and two firms of dealers. Without them Fabergé might be still just as unknown as many a better artist.

You may have gathered that I do not recommend you to start collecting Fabergé, or anybody else who is at the height of his fame (and other people's fortune). Remember Burne-Jones's painting, 'The Golden Stair', which was sold, if my memory serves me rightly, for £35,000 in 1905 and £350 in 1935; not that monetary gain is the be-all of specialist collection, but you like to feel that you are right in the forefront of a new fashion rather than tagging along in the wake. The buyer who paid £35,000 for the 'Golden Stair' could have had everything Picasso had painted up to that date for a tenth of the money. In the same way I would not recommend you, however rich, to start a collection of Paul Lamerie; in the opinion of most people whose opinion is to be respected, he does not in any way excel a dozen other masters of the same or earlier period. You must not attach importance to a name alone, unless you can *see* why. You can *see* that a portrait by Reynolds excels a portrait by Romney, but if you cannot *see* that a ewer by Paul Lamerie excels a ewer by Augustin Courtauld, why pay three times as much for it? They were both master silversmiths employing a number of journey-men,* who no doubt did all the work, for which the master took responsibility by his mark. If you want to collect one maker, any of the names mentioned in Chapter 5 is well worth collecting, and once a collection is in being it enhances the value of that maker. After you have a good collection, all you want in fact, you write a monograph about it and people feel, Aha, I have been missing something.

For the less opulent collector there are many possibilities. I have already suggested the possibilities of a collection of Art Noveau silver, if only for a nest-egg for your great-grandchildren. Of course, it would not merely be silver of

---

* Paul Lamerie left a legacy to two journeymen, on condition that they remained in the employment of his executors long enough to complete the whole of the work in hand at the date of his death.

the period you would collect; it would be fairly important pieces in every way typical of the style and showing in some way the hand of an artist—as designer only, no doubt. Small pieces are likely to be mass-produced, but the larger and more unusual were quite often specially designed by well-known people. One has to consider that the vogue was quite short-lived, not more than twenty years; it has definite roots in the work of William Morris and his colleagues and is a well defined and easily recognizable style. There you have all the elements of a future scarcity-value, whereas at present you can buy at about melting-down price, say thirty important pieces for the price of one helmet-shaped ewer by Lamerie.

Going a little earlier, you might make a collection of the most extravagant mid-Victoriana you can find. After all, look what's happening with the furniture of that period, and look at all the eminent gentlemen who rush to the defence of any mid-Victorian railway station threatened with de-steaming. It could happen with the silver, and at present you can have it at a little below ingot value, because of the cost of breaking up and melting. I would not for myself choose such a collection, but it might be good for laughs for the present, and for the future, who knows? People pay thousands for a Fabergé just as vulgar, and much more recent.

Spoons are a favourite form of special collection, and in the earlier stages the cheapest. In singles or odd lots, spoons back to 1660 can be acquired comparatively cheaply; but as the enthusiasm grows the ambition extends to Tudor or even Plantagenet spoons, where real money is involved. The whole field is perhaps too wide, and it is better to re-strict to an area or a period. For example, the collection of Scottish spoons made by a former Marquess of Breadal-bane was of the utmost value to Sir Charles Jackson in completing his monumental work on makers' marks; with-out that collection, Jackson's Scottish section would have lost half its value to collectors. Again, one might restrict the collection to the period 1800 to 1825, and illustrate with hundreds of examples the transition from Old English to Fiddle. Alternatively, one particular type of spoon, say rat-tailed spoons of all periods; you might become the leading world authority on rat-tailed spoons. The narrower the field you cultivate, the more likely you are to gain distinction.

Silver marked at the minor guilds has great possibilities as a specialist collection, and here you may take any form of plate whatsoever, so long as it has the desired mark. A collection of York plate before 1700 would be of great interest, with its town mark of the half leopard's head and half fleur-de-lis dimidiated. An interesting collection could be formed from any minor guild, as long as the guild is not *so* minor that nothing was marked except spoons. It is best to choose a guild as near as possible; a collector in Devon has far better opportunities of making a good collection of Exeter silver than of Cork. It is quite striking how the products of the minor guilds tend to remain in the immediate vicinity. Generally speaking, such plate may be acquired at very ordinary prices, or even at very low prices, if by chance the mark is not known to 'the trade'. For example, I have acquired a half-dozen of toddy-ladles with the sole mark 'DOUGLAS' at the price of electro-plate, whereas they were without doubt sterling silver made in Aberdeen about 1800. The same sort of thing might very well occur at small sales with early silver of Norwich or Youghal.

It is obviously impossible to rely upon your own chance presence in a shop or an auction room where there may happen to be whatever you have decided to specialize in. You will need to circularize the leading auctioneers throughout the country, stating simply that you are collecting old silver and would like to receive their catalogues when they have such a sale; if the catalogue describes correctly, you are safe enough to send a bid by letter, to save the trouble and cost of travel. You may also circularize antique shops and silver dealers, in this case stating your speciality; they will be very pleased to keep you informed of what they have in stock from time to time and to send you on approval anything you would like to see. Naturally, you are not going to get any wonderful bargains this way, but in time you will get a very good collection, worth a great deal more than the sum of the individual prices you have paid.

There are several excellent year books giving lists of dealers and of auctioneers. It is, of course, better if you can pay at least one visit in person, but there are at least two thousand regular dealers of good status in Great Britain alone. You should not get in touch with more than one dealer in one area, otherwise you may well find two dealers at the same auction running each other up in perfectly good faith, each convinced that he is acting on your instructions. In the case of auctioneers a visit is usually desirable, since by no means do all auctioneers ever handle silver. In the case of one telephone area I have the 'classified trades' edition beside me; and of the two hundred auctioneers listed there is only one who would be of any use to a silver collector, and the one who would be of *most* use is not listed at all. There is little use in writing to auctioneers who only handle livestock or house property. Where you cannot pay a visit it is better to leave your interest in the hands of a local dealer. It is worth keeping in mind that it is in the most remote places that the really 'interesting item' is likely to be found. By 'remote' I do not mean simply 'distant'; the big silver sales in Edinburgh or Dublin are as well attended and get as good prices as most London sales.

To sum up, you will never in a lifetime get together a worth-while specialist collection without the co-operation of a large number of dealers and auctioneers, and in general you are perfectly safe to rely on this; but if it is at all possible, do it yourself.

15

Display and Security

A NUMBER of things have happened since the Marquis of Abercorn used to go shooting in his Star and Riband: nowadays a gala ball means short frocks and dinner jackets, and 'display' is an obscene term to make gamekeepers blench. Nevertheless, the desire to show what you have got is a human and often laudable trait, and the general collector who has followed the precepts of the preceding chapters will be able to show his taste and solvency without indulging in the vulgarity of it.

For the general collector, there can be no such thing as a display cabinet. Everything is to be for use, nothing for show. How distressing to have one's hostess open the display cabinet and after a momentary hesitation take the second-best tea-pot to the kitchen! All such utensils are to be kept in the pantry cupboard or the plate-safe. Let them be brought out as and when required.

Since there is nothing except for use, let's use what we have. Wine coolers, punch-bowls, mentieths, rose-bowls—use them all for flower arrangements, or even let them stand awaiting their flowers. Wine coolers in particular, and some other shapes of vases, are rather difficult to clean inside, and it is a good thing to have a glass liner made to fit. It need not be expensive, a 'scientific glass worker' could make one in ten minutes. The bottom should have a piece of felt or sticking-plaster to prevent scratching—not rubber, which contains sulphur. It is better still to have the inside gilded, but this is fairly expensive. One may, after thorough cleaning, coat the inside with cellulose varnish, as already described; at worst, you can rub the inside with vaseline. Some sort of protection should always be given, for some flower stems leave a stain which is not at all easy to eradicate, and apart from the effort there is silver being rubbed away.

Candlesticks may be stood around in reasonable profusion, but only simple types—if you like ornate ones keep them for the dining-room. Always have candles in them, preferably plain white ones and partially burned. If you have a preference for coloured candles no harm is done, it's a matter of taste; personally I like to see them burnt a little; if you have several colours obviously you must consider the background if you move them around. Place them in useful positions, writing-desks or sidetables; I am unable to give a reason why I don't like them on mantelpieces. A silver-framed wall-mirror with sconces is a magnificent decoration, with uses.

In the dining-room the large Georgian 'stage sideboard' is the ideal medium for keeping your using silver at hand and in view. Candlesticks and fruit-bowl may remain permanently on the table, as may cake-basket, wine coolers and sundry jugs on the sideboard; but sauce-boats, entire dishes and the like should be kept elsewhere until required. A salver or two certainly, but laid flat, never stuck up on edge. The illustration shows a modest dining-room in use; there are sixteen pieces of Georgian silver to be seen here, and with a coffee set and winecoolers there could well be twenty-four without incurring the least odium of ostentation.

Cutlery you can never have too much of. That in daily use is best kept in a cabinet of small drawers in the dining-room—lift-up lids are a nuisance—and it's a good idea to have stops fitted to the back of each drawer so that it cannot be pulled right out and spill its contents on the Crown Derby.

The remaining cutlery should be wrapped in strips of felt and kept in the plate-safe. Never have cutlery loose in a large drawer; it will work itself into a large untidy heap in which one must scrabble for anything wanted; very wrong, though that's how mine is.

A specialist collection is very different. Here there is no suggestion whatever that anything is for use, and in any case the specialist has already a very satisfactory general collection. Here the display cabinet is entirely admissible, and should be very well made and as airtight as possible. Lay some silica gel in the bottom, in a muslin bag if you like, to absorb moisture; in perfectly dry conditions tarnishing is very slow indeed. I prefer cupboards made in wall-alcoves, and I have seen very excellent cabinets made by slapping an opening clean through a partition wall, building a sheet of armour-plate glass immovably into the showing side and having an access from the adjacent room by unscrewing a large sheet of plywood. True, there were forty screws; but then the cabinet was so dry and airtight that there was no need to open it at all for polishing purposes, and it would certainly puzzle the casual burglar.

The best way of keeping any silver is in a plate safe, which is a steel structure about four feet high as a rule, made of $\frac{5}{8}''$ steel, doubled-up at all the corners and having a massive door from which bolts shoot out in all directions. It is lined with baize and has a number of adjustable shelves likewise covered with baize. The lock is so constructed that if it is destroyed by explosive the bolts cannot be withdrawn, and it is certainly far more of a problem for burglars than the ordinary fire-proof safe. It is NOT fire-proof, and for this reason, as well as its weight, is best situated on a stone or concrete floor. It is practically air-tight, and with a little silica gel in bags here and there silver will retain its polish more or less indefinitely in a plate safe. They are not cheap by any means, but one may buy them surprisingly cheaply at 'house' auction sales, the reason being that to fetch it home will cost you from twenty to fifty pounds, according to distance.

The best security, of course, is insurance. Silver is usually insurable at the ordinary domestic rate but the best way to ensure that no doubt will rise in the mind of the assessor is to have a complete inventory and valuation made by a qualified person. If you want to save money you can make the inventory yourself and ask the valuer to check and value each item. Be sure that he understands for what purpose the inventory is being made. The normal fee is based on a percentage of the total value, but most valuers will give an estimate for the job, based on the time they expect it to take, and this is the most favourable when an inventory for insurance is to be made. Never under-insure; values are always rising and a valuation made ten years before a loss may be quite unrealistic.

If the collection is at all valuable it is as well to have the inventory attached to the insurance policy, agreed by the company and kept at your bank. The agreement by the company is not essential in the ordinary way; an assessor would accept an inventory signed by a qualified valuer, as long as there was no suspicion that you had been quietly disposing of the collection.

For a large collection a strong-room is necessary, which is simply a fire-proof room lined with baize-covered steel shelves and fitted with a steel door, burglar-proofed according to the timidity of the owner.

If the collection is properly insured, and adequately stowed, the owner may sleep quietly of nights or take a voyage round the world, without a care on his mind. One hears of very rich men with armed guards, electrified wires, guard dogs and similar horrors, but this is making a nightmare of what should be a permanent pleasure. There is very little that the ordinary collector of silver cannot replace, somewhere, somehow, with money; leave that worry to the insurance company, and meantime enjoy your collection to the full.

16

Care and Repair

'SILVER NEEDS such a lot of cleaning' is a myth which still deters many potential collectors. Once it was true, now no longer. The factors which cause tarnishing are not nearly so common, and entirely new methods of cleaning and keeping clean have come into use.

Ordinary tarnishing is caused by sulphur compounds, which occur in the atmosphere as a product of combustion. In the last century millions of chimneys, factory and domestic, belched black smoke into the air, open fires blazed on every hearth, and lighting was by burning gas, oil or candle; so that the whole atmosphere of towns, and the interiors of even country houses, were equally laden with visible smoke and invisible sulphur compounds. It was inevitable that in those days much time had to be spent in the pantry.

Today, from a vantage-point in London from which you could have seen a million smoking chimneys at the turn of the century, the only sign of combustion is a wisp of white over Battersea. The internal combustion engine has taken over the job of polluting the atmosphere, but even a badly adjusted Diesel cannot compare with a coal fire in tarnishing power. In the home, electric lighting is almost universal, central heating is common, electrical heating is everywhere and gas fires are completely ventilated. Only with the oil-burning heater are the products of combustion left in the room.

Silver kept in an air-tight case or a plate safe will never

tarnish, although it is usual to rub it up periodically with a dry chamois leather. Individual pieces may be stored in clean plastic bags, sealed to exclude air, and incidentally preventing scratching. Similarly the atmosphere of the rooms in which you keep your silver should be clean and dry; tarnishing takes place much more quickly in a damp atmosphere. If your house is lighted by electricity and heated by any modern method, you have nothing to worry about. If you have an atavistic feeling for an open fire make sure it draws well, and if possible burn wood in preference to coal. Oil-burning room heaters are to be avoided as they leave all the products of combustion in the room and also produce considerable humidity—in the region of a pint of water for every gallon of paraffin consumed.

Atmospheric tarnishing shows itself first as a slight dulling of the polish, succeeded by a yellowish tinge and then by a blackish-grey veining which gradually spreads into patches and finally covers the whole surface in black, with a kind of gun-metal glint in it. It is usual to clean silver at the first sign of yellowing, but the same methods serve after longer neglect.

There is no 'best' way of cleaning silver, but many good ones. The traditional methods are laborious, but in my view leave the best surface, the deep lustre so much to be ad-admired. The best butler I ever had used to wash his silver in warm soapy water and set it on a towel to drip. Then he would rub it with jeweller's rouge on a large dry cheese-cloth. Next he brushed out the chasing with a dry brush and finished off with a large, thin, soft chamois leather. The best table-maid I ever had used to dampen Goddard's plate powder with equal parts of water and methylated spirits, rubbing this all over her silver and brushing it into the chasing with her 'dirty' brush; she then brushed it all over with her 'clean' brush and finished off with a soft yellow duster. Both methods were perfectly satisfactory. The principle is gentle friction with the mildest possible abrasive. Plate powder is now available in bottles as a sort of cream, no doubt the same powder in suspension, and this is very convenient and economical when only a small quantity is required. It is used in the same way, care being taken to brush out the chasing thoroughly and leave quite dry.

While these traditional methods, in loving and expert hands, are perhaps the most desirable, modern research has produced a number of cleaners, polishers and preservers of the greatest interest and usefulness. Their advantages and limitations should be fully understood and they should be used strictly for the purposes for which they are intended. Used intelligently they have quite reformed the care of silver. They fall into two main groups: those in which a chemical combines with the sulphides of tarnish and removes them, and those which leave a coating to prevent or delay later tarnishing.

Among the first type is a tarnish-removing liquid into which the silver is dipped for a few seconds; it is useful for any kind of silver, but invaluable for deeply-chased pieces or food-stained cutlery. This 'Dip' is a cleaner, not a polisher, and silver thus cleaned must be washed and rubbed up with a polishing-cloth. Dip must not be brought in contact with other metals, many of which it stains black, so be wary about using it where plating has been worn through, and don't splash it about. Even stainless steel may be stained. Good housewives keep a half-gallon jar always handy; it can last as long as two years.

Another innovation is 'Silver Foam', a cleaner-polisher in a quick-to-use form which is very convenient for small jobs and safe with all metals it's likely to meet, so that it can be kept beside the washing-up sink for any odd job.

For more serious tarnishing, an impregnated cotton-wool called 'Duraglit' is very effective. It is made in two types, one for silver and one for brass, so be sure you have the right one. It is quite cheap and can be used liberally, discarding each 'pull' as it becomes black; wear gloves, by the way. After cleaning a heavily-tarnished piece by this method the colour of the silver may still not be all that one could wish, but after a few weeks of the ordinary routine it will be as perfect as if it had never been neglected.

Silver in regular use, being washed and dried, scarcely needs any formal cleaning at all, but it is advisable to go over everything periodically and thoroughly. Between these inspections the use of an impregnated cloth for drying washed silver-ware and for dusting and rubbing-up other items in daily use will keep them in beautiful condition without any extra labour. Such a cloth can be prepared at home quite simply: add two tablespoonfuls of ammonia and one tablespoonful of Goddards Plate Powder to half a pint of water. Soak a good drying-up cloth in this mixture and hang up to drip dry. Its efficiency will last about a fortnight, when the cloth should be washed, dried and re-dipped.

But these indefatigable scientists are not content with making silver-cleaning easy; they want to do away with it altogether, and they are succeeding.

There is a type of polish called 'Long Term' which is absolutely correctly named. Silver is cleaned in the ordinary way then polished with 'Long Term'; in addition to polishing it leaves a completely imperceptible coating which prevents tarnishing for a considerable time, especially if the piece is not handled a great deal or rubbed with impregnated polishing cloths. Under favourable conditions the term may be a year; under very bad conditions, in a test I conducted personally, slight tarnish first showed after three months. Under similar conditions with ordinary polish the same amount of tarnish showed in four days. 'Long Term' may be used with any silver, but obviously its value is greatest on all those things exposed to air but not being constantly handled. Silver in regular use does not need this treatment, and the effect is rather short-lived; but for candlesticks, vases, wine coolers, cake-baskets and fixed silver such as wall-sconces it is simply invaluable. (It *is* rather expensive.)

There is even a further development—a Permanent Polish. This is not a do-it-yourself job. You must arrange with your silversmith to send it away for this to be done. The process consists of bringing the silver to a perfect polish, chemically clean, then applying a highly-developed synthetic resin by a carefully-controlled process. The result is a beautiful polish, stated to be completely permanent. From the experience of a relative, I know that the polish is quite unimpaired after a period of years; and from my own extensive experience of such resins in another sphere I have every reason to believe that here at last is the Permanent Polish. It is expensive, but it is once only; and it makes possible the display of all those intricate pieces which have almost disappeared, from the sheer impossibility of finding the labour to clean them.

All these modern developments completely dispel the idea that a collection of silver entails many hours of labour. It sometimes seems to me that none of those wonderful and easy processes produce quite the deep, glowing lustre got by loving labour and plate powder, but this is probably imagination or prejudice. In any case, what housewife is going to sacrifice the advantage of cleaning her candlesticks once a year for the sake of a scarcely perceptible tinge?

Whatever method is used, always be gentle. Silver is a soft metal and of later years tends to be used too thin. On corners, on gadrooning, on any protuberance, it is all too easy to rub right through after a generation of thoughtless enthusiasm. Especially is this true of Sheffield Plate, where the surface silver may be as little as one thousandth of an inch in thickness, compared with about a hundredth in small, light, solid silver. The thickness of electro-plating is something from which I avert the mind.

The thing to remember always is that this beautiful surface must never be broken or scratched. No abrasive harsher than plate powder should ever be used, nor any brush harder than the traditional plate brush. Agreed, somehow there is always an old tooth brush in the pantry, but make sure it is bristle, not nylon. I once came upon a 'casual help' attacking a George I coffee-pot with a pad of steel wool. My remarks had a moral tendency, the moral being that really good silver should be attended by yourself in person, or else by fully competent and reliable domestics. Especially does this apply to 'Britannia standard' silver, so much softer than the ordinary standard and with an even whiter and lovelier lustre; and to silver-gilt, which should never be cleaned at all. It does not tarnish. If it appears dull, this is only grime which may be removed with warm water and detergent, drying off with a very soft cloth.

When rubber has been in contact with silver the sulphiding is more concentrated than by atmosphere, but will usually yield to the 'dip' or the impregnated cotton-wool, though some patience may be necessary. I once had pointed out to me a number of difficult black marks on the inside bottom of a large rose bowl, which was in fact being used for roses; it turned out that the flower arranger had a wire affair to aid her art, fixed to the bottom by rubber suckers. When silver vessels are used for flowers—and there can be nothing better—it is a good plan to fill the inside with a polythene bag first of all, so that water, stems or wires do not come in contact with the silver at all.

Chlorine and some acids tarnish silver very seriously, the first usually in the form of common salt, the second as vinegar, in sauces for example. The corrosion so produced is a dull-grey colour, and the surface is slightly granular, the fine polish being destroyed. Table appointments such as salt-cellars or mustard-pots often have glass liners, which give complete protection; or the interior is gilt, which is perfectly effective until in time it wears through; it should then be re-gilded, or, as a poorish substitute, a clear cellulose lacquer may be used. Bowls of salt-spoons should be gilt; if not they must not be left in the salt but washed up after every meal with the other cutlery. Sauce-boats and ladles must also be washed, for the ingredients will cause discoloration and eventually corrosion, although not so quickly as salt.

It sometimes happens that by some neglect silver becomes thus corroded, or you may even buy it in this state. There is nothing to be done about Sheffield Plate, because there will be no silver under the corrosion; but in most solid silver it is a matter of surfacing and burnishing, much as if it were a new piece. I could give directions for doing this, but it would not be a good service. If you are a competent silversmith you don't need directions, and if you aren't you'll make a botch of it and blame me. Turn it in to your local silversmith and he will send it to Birmingham to be re-surfaced by experts with every facility at hand. Nobody who has not experienced it can imagine the pleasure when a dented and corroded bit of junk comes back a handsome piece of plate. The pleasure may possibly be mitigated by the bill, but it's usually worth it. In general, for all ordinary silver from mid-eighteenth century onwards, I advise having it kept in the best repair. Cracks and dents take away all the pleasure, and the value too. In the case of rare and valuable pieces, certainly everything before 1720, expert advice should be sought before ordering repairs. In many cases it is better to leave it alone. A prospective purchaser will always be very suspicious about any signs of repair, particularly in the vicinity of the hall-mark. In any case, when repairs are made to a piece of any importance, it is advisable to have an invoice from the repairer detailing exactly what has been done; this should be kept with the inventory.

Additions and alterations are seldom advisable. I once

I

bought at auction a number of George III plates, gadroon edges, very handsome. Much later, an acute observer expressed the opinion that the gadrooning was a Victorian addition, and a tiny hall-mark for 1884 was found in the pattern. I sold the plates, for more than I paid for them, but nothing like so much as if the Victorian owner had been content to let the original edges alone. I have a George II sauce-boat, originally quite plain, lovely little thing, but some later owner had the body chased and decorated, no doubt according to the taste of the time but spoiling it for future generations. So don't alter, don't embellish; keep it as the silversmith left it, that your children may call you blessed. Silver may well last thousands of years, and however much money you may have paid you are still a trustee for posterity.

Appendix I

Glossary

Alloy: The only alloy used with silver is copper, the Standard being 18 pennyweights of copper to 11 oz. 2 dwts. of pure silver. Pure silver is too soft for use, and any other metal used as an alloy makes the silver too brittle.

Antimonial silver: See dyscrasite.

Argent: The heraldic term for silver.

Argentite: A dark grey silver sulphide, $Ag_2 S$.

Assay: To test silver for its standard of purity.

Assay Master: The principal of the Assay Office; a sworn officer of great responsibility.

Assay Office: The place where the assay is conducted.

Bar-and-bead: An edge decoration, self-descriptive.

Bead: An edge decoration of raised dots.

Bismuth silver: See chilenite and schapbachite.

Black silver: See stephanite.

Bleeding: The copper base showing through the silver coating in Sheffield Plate.

Britannia metal: An alloy of tin, copper and antimony, used sometimes to imitate silver but more usually as a base for electro-plating, E.P.B.M.

Britannia standard: The term often used for the higher standard of silver enacted in 1696, allowing only 10 dwts. copper in the pound weight of silver. Compulsory from 1697 to 1720, permissive ever since. From the figure of Britannia being one of the hall-marks enacted.

Brittle silver ore: See stephanite.

Chasing: Ornamenting by raising and indenting.

Chilenite: An ore, silver bismuthid, Ag_6 Bi.

Cocus-wood: A dense West Indian wood widely used for handles.

Cupel: A small porous crucible used in assaying.

Diet: In assaying, the assayer is allowed to remove eight grains per pound weight of silver, of which four grains is allowed to be lost, and the other four grains reserved as the diet, in the diet-box. (From *dies*, a day.)

Diet-box: The carefully locked box in which the diet is preserved. It is opened at intervals by a committee, and the diet assayed to prove the average standard assayed during the period. The silver then becomes part of the income of the Assay Office.

Engraving: The process of decorating silver by incising, the lines being cut directly into the silver.

Flatting Mill: A device, invented in 1727, for reducing silver to the required thickness by rollers; much cheaper than the former method of hammering, and left the metal much more ductile. Now universally used.

Fly-press: A device used in the eighteenth century and since for stamping small or medium articles to shape, for example bowls; operated by hand aided by a fly-wheel. Superseded by the power-press.

Foil: Silver beaten to the thinnest possible, one thousandth of an inch; also called leaf.

Gadroon: An edge decoration, sometimes called pie-crust.

German silver: An alloy similar to nickel silver (q.v.) but with less nickel.

Graver: The tool used for engraving.

Guild: A fraternity of craftsmen incorporated by a Royal Charter.

Hall Marks: The marks ordained by Act of Parliament to be

stamped on assayed silver; from Goldsmith's *Hall*, where the assay was conducted.

King's Pattern: A decoration for spoons, basically as Queen's pattern, but more ornate, having a raised decoration along the centre of the shank. Middle and late Victorian.

Leaf: Silver leaf is beaten out like gold leaf, but much thicker; 1,000 to the inch in silver, 250,000 to the inch in gold. Also called foil.

Liner: An interior fitment of blue glass, made to fit, used with pierced-work silver, also with mustard-pots, salt-cellars and the like, to avoid corrosion.

Mock silver: An alloy of copper, tin, nickel and zinc.

Mosaic silver: An alloy of tin, mercury and bismuth.

Nickel silver: An alloy of nickel, zinc and copper, extensively used as a base for electro-plating, E.P.N.S.

Niello: A decorative system in which a pattern is cut out of the surface of silver and emphasized with black, composed of an alloy of silver, lead, copper, bismuth and sulphur. Developed in Italy in the fifteenth century, used widely in the nineteenth century, especially in France and Russia. Russian work usually called tula.

Old English: A design of spoon, completely plain and very elegant. Eighteenth century.

Proustite: A red ore of silver, arsenic and sulphur, $Ag_3 As S_3$.

Pyrargarite: An ore of silver, antimony and sulphur, $Ag_3 Sb S_3$.

Pyx: Originally the casket in which the Host was reserved in Roman Catholic altar service; later the casket in which the officers of the Mint deposited one or more of the coins minted daily. At intervals these were melted down and assayed, to prove the integrity of the officers. This was known as 'the trial of the pyx' and was formerly a solemn ceremony in the presence of the Lord

Chamberlain and the Privy Council. It is now discontinued. The term pyx is sometimes incorrectly applied to the diet-box (q.v.).

Queen's pattern: A decoration for spoons, consisting of a shell at the base and a raised line on each side of the shank. Early Victorian.

Rat-tailed: A form of spoon in which the handle is prolonged under the bowl in the form of a tail.

Red silver (dark): See pyrargarite.

Red silver (light): See proustite.

Regency: Properly the period 1811 to 1820, but often applied to silver made under the Graeco-classical influence between 1795 and 1825. It is therefore to be regarded as applying to the style rather than the precise period.

Ruby silver ore: See proustite.

Schapbachite: A grey ore containing lead, silver, bismuth and sulphur, $Pb\ Ag_2\ Bi_2\ S_5$.

Silver red: A pigment, silver chromate.

Silver glance: See argentite.

Silverling: A coin mentioned in the Bible, Isaiah vii, 23; probably a bekah, half a shekel.

Silver powder: An alloy of bismuth, tin and mercury, powdered; used in lacquer-work.

Silver sand: Fine white sand, containing no silver.

Silver solder: An alloy of silver and tin.

Silver steel: An alloy containing a modicum of silver.

Snarling iron: A tool used in beating silver vessels internally.

Spun silver: (1) A thread made by spinning a silver ribbon round a cotton core. (2) Silver shaped from the sheet on the lathe; a process much used since 1760.

Stephanite: A black ore containing silver, antimony and sulphur, $Ag_5\ Sb\ S_4$.

Touch: The operation of testing silver by the touchstone; obsolete. Also applied to the hall-mark or the operation of applying the hall-mark.

APPENDIX I 135

Touchstone: A hard black stone used in early assaying; quite good with gold, but very rough-and-ready with silver; superseded long ago by cupellation and chemical methods.

Tula: see Niello.

Appendix II

Weights, ancient and modern

TROY weight (derived from Troyes in France, a former silver-working centre) is the weight used for all gold and silver.

1 pound = 12 ounces = 240 pennyweights = 5,760 grains. The usual denomination is the ounce, whatever the weight. Thus a wine cistern in the Mulliner collection is described as weighing 308 ozs. 10 dwts.

1 ounce Troy = 480 grains = 31·10 grammes metric.

AVOIRDUPOIS weight is used for everything EXCEPT gold and silver. There is no simple conversion. Troy weights or balances should always be used. If in emergency avoirdupois weights must be used, conversion is as follows:

To convert pounds avoirdupois to pounds Troy, multiply by 175 and divide by 144.

To convert ounces avoirdupois to ounces Troy, multiply by 175 and divide by 192.

TOWER weight, the standard in medieval Europe, and in England until 1926:

1 pound = 20 shillings = 240 pence = 5,400 grains. The pound and the penny were therefore about 6 per cent less than the pound and the pennyweight Troy.
1 shilling = 270 grains, therefore about 12 per cent MORE than half an ounce Troy.

In considering at least the larger articles stated in this weight, if one disregards the pence, calls the shillings half-ounces and the pounds twelve ounces, this gives a very fair idea of the massiveness or otherwise of each piece. Thus in chapter 8 the 'broad covered ewer weighing fifteen pounds three shillings and eightpence' would by this rough method be about 180 ounces, and the twelve spoons mentioned later would be 2 ounces each. One has thus an idea what they would look like; if it is necessary to have exactitude, one can work it out from the tables above.

ANCIENT (Hebrew, Babylonian, Egyptian.)

The principal weights were the shekel and the talent.
1 Shekel = 258 grains = 16·72 grammes metric.
3,000 shekels = 1 talent = approx 120 lbs. Troy = approx 50·15 kilograms.
Other weights:

20 gerah = 1 shekel
2 bekah = 1 shekel
100 shekels = 1 maneh
30 maneh = 1 talent.

There is some dubiety about the value of the maneh; it has been stated at 60 shekels, and 50 maneh to the talent, which also gives 3,000 shekels to the talent. The maneh is seldom met with.

It will be understood that with weights used over a period of thousands of years there were local variations both in place and time, just as the acre was a different area formerly in England, Scotland and Ireland, and the gallon is a different measure in the United States than in England. The table given is an average which may be used with confidence, for example, over the whole period covered by the Old Testament. (For the New Testament, use the Greek tables.) As a ready guide, think of a shekel as a good half-ounce and a talent as a hundredweight, More exactly:

Shekels to ounces Troy, multiply by 43 and divide by 80.
Talents to ounces Troy, multiply by 1440.

CLASSICAL—Greek.

100 drachmae = 1 mina = 1 pound Troy.
60 minae = 1 talent = 60 pounds Troy.

There are many other weights, such as the obol, one
eighth of a drachma, better known as coins; and others such
as the tetradrachm, self-explanatory. This table gives the
essentials, and exhaustive tables can be found in any classical
dictionary.

CLASSICAL—Roman.

1 uncia = 420 grains = 27·22 grammes.
12 uncia = 1 *as* = 10½ ounces Troy.
100 *as*   = 1 centumpondium = 87½ pounds Troy, commonly called one Roman Talent.

As with the Greek weights, there are many divisions and
multiples of weights, many used for other goods, and many
more familiar as coinage, such as the denarius (about one-
seventh of an uncia). The *as* of copper was an extremely
ancient Roman currency, used from the Founding of the
City. During the early days of the Republic, the uncia of
silver was reckoned as the equivalent of 70 *as* of copper.
During the opulence of the Empire, the uncia was little
used, and silver was reckoned by the *as*.

If one thinks of the uncia as an ounce, of the *as* as a
pound, and of the talent as half a hundredweight, one has a
fair idea of these weights. To convert the *as*, the most usual
weight met with, into ounces Troy, multiply by 10·5.

While Greek ideas and language were widely favoured
by the Romans from the First Century onwards, there was a
marked reluctance to use other than Roman weights in
Italy. Greek weights were generally in use throughout the
Eastern parts of the Empire.

DARK AGES. When weights are mentioned these are usually Roman, the *as* being translated as pound. With seldom any central authority, weights varied by place and time. Thus in the reign of Louis X of France the pound was 16 ounces at Paris, but only 13½ at Toulouse, and 13 at Marseilles; in Lyons it was 14 ounces, but 15 ounces when weighing silk. One can only imagine the difficulties at an earlier period. Gradually the Tower weight became fairly standard throughout Western Europe, until superseded by Troy.

It is not my business to propound an ideal system of weights for silver, only to state the weights at present in use and formerly in use and to indicate simple means whereby the modern reader can form an intelligent conception of the old weights. It's much required: very recently an intelligent and educated person expressed the view that a talent was 'about five shillings' worth of silver'.

*   *   *

For most of the photographs illustrating this book I am indebted to the curator and trustees of the Holburne of Menstrie Museum of Art, Bath; to Garrard & Co., Ltd., London; and to C. T. Gilmer, Ltd., of Bath. By their kindness I have been enabled to show a collection of photographs of the greatest interest to collectors, none of which, as far as I am aware, has hitherto been published. I must also thank *Ideal Home* for the photographs of my dining-room.

Not having spent much of my life in a pantry, I had to be greatly assisted in Chapter 16, on the care of silver. I have particularly to thank Mr. Thornton, of J. Goddard & Sons Ltd., who was so kind as to read the whole of a transcript of the chapter and comment on it; Mr. Sherlock of Garrard & Co., Ltd., for information about the Permanent Polish; my daughter, Viscountess Prestwood, who practically re-wrote the chapter; and Lady Alison Davis, for the recipe for an impregnated polishing-cloth.

J.H.

Index